To Melissa — 9/2/23

May This book inspire you to greater levels of your own dance in life and in your body & soul. So great to meet you, in the dance of life,

Françoise

Movement
for the Mind®

DANCE THAT AWAKENS
HEALING, INSPIRATION & WISDOM

by Françoise E. Netter

Graphic design: Dasha Jensen.
Cover photo: mythja/shutterstock.com

Printed in the United States of America

ISBN: 978-1-4823-6804-8 (paperback)
ISBN: 978-1-63002-708-7 (Kindle ebook)
ISBN: 978-1-4524-7890-6 (Barnes & Noble ebook, Smashwords ebook)
Library of Congress Control Number: 2013903536
BISAC: Body, Mind & Spirit / Inspiration & Personal Growth

Published by: Pathways Press
            P.O. Box 18732
            Boulder, Colorado 80308

Movement for the Mind® is a registered trademark by Françoise E. Netter.

Some names have been changed to protect the anonymity of the individuals mentioned in this book.

Praise for Movement of the MInd

"Françoise Netter is a master of her craft. She has designed a methodology that allows the full vibrant being to emerge in each of us. We forget how incredible the body is—how able it is to heal itself, and when we merge the mind, body, spirit through movement, amazing things happen. As a recipient of Françoise's work, I highly recommend this book to anyone in a body!"

— *Kathleen Jacoby, Author, Vision of the Grail*

"Françoise Netter is a first class teacher who has written a first class book. The book is a worthy compliment to the excellence she brings to the classroom. It teaches readers to trust their feelings, their bodies and their minds. It empowers them to take risks and realize the positive results which risk taking often brings. Dance and movement in the book are treated as metaphors for the larger lessons we must all learn in life. Namely, to connect all the creative forces within us to the greater spiritual forces comprising our universe."

—*Jay Wissot, Ph.D., President, Colorado Consulting Services*

"Movement for the Mind provides a readable and very complete description of the many uses of movement to promote well-being in just about every aspect of our personal, creative and work lives. Netter's stories are captivating and inspirational, giving the reader a sense of "I can do this!" Movement moves from the possibly unreachable realm of the dancer to the attainable everyday realm of all of us. I can see Netter's book being immensely useful to artists, executives, healers, therapists, teachers of young and old, and those of us who are looking for an enjoyable way to relax, heal or fine tune some aspect of our being in our everyday work or personal life."

—*Dr. Lorna Catford, Ph.D., Co-Author, The Path of the Everyday Hero*

"THIS IS A MUST READ FOR EDUCATORS! As an educator, reading Movement for the Mind is a breath of fresh air! It serves as a reminder that happiness comes through connection of mind and body. This book reminds you how to reconnect to your world and to find inner creativity and passion! ...It teaches educators the value of movement in the classroom to help youth find and express their own creativity and sense of individuality. What a great tool this technique of movement serves in an educational setting and as an outlet for anyone needing to re-establish balance and connection between the body and mind! Movement for the Mind is a must read for educators of all ages!"

– Molly Kinghorn, Educator

"Personally, I feel that I have a whole paradigm shift concerning dance and the mind due to this book. Movement for the Mind has left me excited to try out and utilize these new techniques to deal with old issues, to become less stressed and more energetic and to ultimately become more healthy in body and mind ... this book has made me realize that I can create my own choreography and dance to the beat of my own drum and in the process, connect with my mind and open to a whole new way of thinking and living!"

—Teresa Bauer, Teacher

"After reading Movement for the Mind and working with the principles, I learned that this work is a very valuable tool for many reasons. Children who are shy suddenly are not shy anymore. They feel secure enough to trust their own bodies and respond to the feelings that movement evokes. Additionally, those boys that think its silly to move and connect did so in a very positive manner. Overall, this journey has made it possible to trust myself more, connect to something deep inside and gave me a sense of freedom and purpose in my classroom."

—Angela Blakeslee, Educator

"This process of movement gave me back my life. The two years I spent doing Movement for the Mind with you allowed me to learn about my tapestry inside and to hold on to it…I learned that I first have to create the space for things that I desire inside before I can ever hope to manifest them on the outside."

—Betty, Psychologist

"Françoise, thank you so very much for sharing your work and passion with me. I believe that using this material has the potential to change untold lives for the better. Reading Movement for the Mind, especially Chapter Six: Dance as Physical Healing, has changed my life. Applying the principles in Movement for the Mind and working with the Magic of Movement CD helped me address my fears and create a healing break-through… I look forward to working with my colleagues to incorporate this into our professional lives, with my wife to incorporate it into our private lives and to simply work with it alone to establish better balance in my life."

—Daniel Draper, Coach

"Working with my body through Movement for the Mind is healing and has helped integrate different aspects of myself. I loved your energy, enthusiasm, humor and holistic perspective that you bring to this work in this book."

— *Pete, Whole Life Expo Participant*

Dedication

This book treats dance as a metaphor for life. It is an invitation to reclaim our creative connection to the body, and to use movement as a purposeful and joyous process for integrating body, mind, emotions, and spirit and solving the problems we once thought of as only mental. For some it will be a call for healing. For others it is an opportunity to express feelings in the body for the first time. For many it might just be the invitation to embrace the forgotten child and artist within. I believe that there is an inner dancer in each of us, and I dedicate this book to that universal and conscious place.

Table of Contents

Foreword

For twenty-five years others and I taught the Personal Creativity in Business course at the Stanford University Graduate School of Business. And then and ever since it has been offered by a growing group of teachers not only at Stanford but at other schools, in corporations and for nonprofit groups and individuals who need this kind of awakening and support of their inherent creativity to deal with the challenges and opportunities of their lives.

For much of that time, Françoise Netter and her dance and movement work have been an integral part of this effort. Why? Because you cannot be consistently creative and lead life to the fullest without engaging not just the mind, but also the heart, the spirit and the body. The last aspect, body, is tricky, yet essential to unlocking the rest for all of us on various times on our journey if it is to be a creative one.

Françoise is a master at what she does. Gifted and a professional. Unique. Like only a few of the visitors and contributors to our class, she sat in it as a participant in order to make sure that what she was doing was of maximum impact to our students. She engaged their bodies in dance and movement in a way that led to breakthroughs and tools that stayed with people.

And now she has translated that brilliance and care to this book for you to use and grow in ways you can't imagine.

When Françoise came for a class it was always a little exciting, maybe even scary for some of the students. We were going to dance in a graduate business class? To keep them guessing and make it light, I would sometimes play a recording of the song, "Dancing Cheek to Cheek," as they entered the room. But Françoise changed the mood step by step. First we (I always participated) were guided to an awareness of our body. Then we explored movement and what it meant in terms of who we are at our core and what our life purpose is. We were transformed during one session. Students spoke with a sort of wonder about what just happened. They followed up by integrating that experience with the other more traditional work they were getting in the class.

This book gives you a chance to have that same kind of experience but to have it in a sustained way in various parts of your life and to meet almost any challenge. In our Stanford class we were focusing on awakening the body-mind-heart-spirit connection for leading a creative life, making your life itself a work of art. This book goes beyond and deeper, however, in the sense that Françoise guides you through her work with stress, psychotherapy and physical healing as well as creativity. You may have worked with each one of these life challenges in many different ways and successfully. But try engaging your body-mind connection with the exercises and approaches in this book and you might be surprised at the new levels you will achieve—breakthroughs instead of stress, support for healing, awakened creative energy, and new understanding and control of your personality based on your highest self.

You can read this book straight through and get something from the stories Françoise tells and the new perspective she offers. But you'll get an order of magnitude more from it if you engage with the exercises, if you bring this kind of movement into your life. It takes effort at first. But once you get the basic exercise down, you have a tool that you can use in other parts of the book and whenever you need it.

So I suggest that you get the basic exercise first and then go to the chapter that represents a major challenge for you, be it stress, creativity, mental issues, or healing. Do the movement work in every chapter. See what happens. Pay attention. Keep at it with what works for you. Use this book as a guide to a full, rich life from every aspect of your being.

—*Michael Ray, John G. McCoy-Banc One Professor of Creativity and Innovation (Emeritus) Stanford Business School and Author, Creativity in Business and The Highest Goal.*

Acknowledgments

Giving thanks and gratitude seems like the best place to complete a project. This book is no exception. I'd like to thank Jill Schettler for first believing in this work and for holding my hand patiently through the dramas of much of the editorial process. Thank you to Michael Ray and Lorna Catford for their support, encouragement, and enthusiasm, and for always participating in the "dance." Michael has been a friend, a mentor, and an inspiration in both how he lives his life and in the creative work that he has brought to Stanford University and to the world.

I'd like to express gratitude to all of my friends whose support, encouragement, and love is unmatcheable. Thanks to Patrick, who helped me painstakingly with my computer, so I could first write. A special thanks to Kathy who told me I "had" to write this book, and encouraged me with her loving insights and not so subtle proddings. Thanks to my mother, Ilse and brother, Patrick for paving the way as authors. Thanks to my cat, Mahali, who kept me company while I wrote, and sat on most pages of the manuscript. Thanks to Thayer and Paul, Jeanne and Mark, and to Dave C. for providing me with havens away from home to write.

Thanks to all of my students and clients over the past thirty plus years. Without their trust, courage, and willingness to "dance" on this path, this book would not exist. I'd like to thank my teachers and mentors in dance and dance therapy, and those who believed in and pioneered the field of dance and creative movement.

Thanks to Phil Tobias who not only "told" me this book had to get out, but generously helped create the product that could be distributed.

Finally, I'd like to thank my spiritual teachers and the path of Siddha Yoga for bringing me to the wellspring and wisdom of my soul.

Introduction

*"I think the reason dance has held such an ageless magic
or the world is that it has been the symbol
of the performance for living."*

— *Martha Graham*

This original manuscript was written over ten years ago,
however as I spent time re-editing and updating various sections,
the contents seem more significant and relevant than ever.

I just finished conducting a graduate credit course for educators
on Movement for the Mind: Integrating right and left brain learning.
Teachers continually share with me their frustration with the learning
environment and concern for their students and tell me that there is an
imminent need for both balance and integration in the classroom and
curriculum. My courses on Movement, Motivation, Yoga and Creativity
are extraordinarily popular. Educators are realizing that without
inspiration and utilizing a wide variety of creative modalities including
creative movement to engage students, learning is just not happening.
The compartmentalization and segmentation that I describe and refer
to in this book about our modern 21st century society are only too
apparent in our educational systems. Even in primary schools, PE and
the Arts are labeled "Specials" and are only intermittently available each
week. There is rampant diagnosis of ADD and ADHD and lack of focus
and concentration is a serious impediment to learning. The principles
and exercises described in this book address solutions than can be
profoundly implemented in educational venues for children and for
adults who never got this form of "education."

The information in this book I believe offers a unique
antidote to many of the problems facing us today. It integrates body
with mind and creates a vehicle for learning, fun, creativity and
revelation. It incorporates the principles of "The Secret," "Shadow

Work" and utilizes as a vehicle what we all share in common: our bodies and minds. It is akin to Yoga and to what the ancient Yogis instruct us about life; that the treasures that we all are looking for are always there, right in front of us or more precisely, within us.

While I was in graduate school, a living disciple of Isadora Duncan, who was a guest lecturer at the school, was asked, "Do you think Isadora Duncan would have recommended Dance Therapy?" She answered, "Isadora believed that if every child was taught the principles of dance, there would be no need for therapy."

This book will show you how to apply movement as a powerful technique for creativity, problem solving, healing, and personal growth by combining two of our most precious resources — the body and the mind. While there are numerous techniques available that stimulate the body/mind connection, Movement for the Mind is unique in that its foundation is rooted in both art and mental awareness. By incorporating movement principles that are easily learned and then expanded upon with directed mental imagery, you will learn how to actively create what you want and to use each session as a practice field for life. Furthermore, you will tap into an ancient calling for self-expression and joy that is found in the most basic use of this body — dance/movement.

Whether you are an educator seeking to integrate right and left brain learning in your classroom, a working professional seeking stress management, someone who is ill and suffering from chronic pain, someone who is seeking greater peace and clarity in your life emotionally and spiritually, or someone who just wants to expand your creativity — this book can offer you an expanded vision and experience. For those of you who have already experienced the aesthetic delight of movement, this book will teach you how to combine a sense of purpose and mental clarity with your movements allowing you to design dances that can teach, heal or simply exhilarate.

In an age that is dominated by the intellect and technology, this technique of moving mindfully takes you deeper into your psyche and at the same time allows you to safely re-connect to your body. Connecting to the body while focusing the mind allows you to capture the moment and pause in a space that can align you physically, mentally, emotionally, and spiritually. This experience of internal alignment causes profound insights, and can lead to significant physical and behavioral changes.

Because the technique is largely internally directed, the fear of being watched or compared to others is eliminated. This allows you to discover a personal freedom in your body that you may have reserved only for childhood. Each person's experience is unique and yet universal themes such as feeling relaxed, energized, enthusiastic, alive, more aware, and connected are shared by individuals of all ages and from all walks of life.

Movement for the Mind can be practiced individually or in a group session and can also be used to strengthen communication and enhance relationships. Yet even in a group session, each individual has an opportunity to connect to what is personally significant.

For example, in a group session sponsored by a private corporation to enhance creativity in the work place, one executive abandoned his resistance to "dancing" and discovered that the tools for creativity and communication could be explored and enhanced significantly through Movement for the Mind.

Through a process that allowed him to substitute movement for words, he first learned to listen to the flows and rhythms in his own body starting with the breath and then learned how to explore some of his work patterns and his communication skills with others.

In the session he practiced new ways of moving that also reflected the mental images of creativity that he desired. At the end of the session he shared, "I had no idea that I could learn this much about myself and others through this method of movement. Not only did I gain an awareness about my work patterns, but also I was able to experience how it felt to be in a creative state and to literally move from this place. I feel great and I have some very useful information that I can apply at work and in my personal life."

Restoring a sense of wholeness and safety in the body is the result that Janice, a woman in her forties, gained from private Movement for the Mind sessions. Janice spent most of her life trying to hide and appear invisible identifying herself as a nice person that never made waves, rarely took risks, and played it safe in all situations over which she had control.

In the sessions, she discovered that the key to her fears and many of her self-limiting beliefs stemmed from wounds from her past. Engaging the body and mind through Movement for the Mind allowed her to experience feelings and memories that she had buried, safely expressing and releasing them, and to make new choices. To her amazement, she discovered a bubbly, animated, and very expressive personality who loved to move and had no need to disappear or remain anonymous.

For Janice making these changes in her body transformed her world from drab to dazzling colors in every area of her life — affecting her physical appearance, her job, and her relationship with her husband and children. The outer changes were significant, but for her, the most profound change was in her inner experience. "I am finally at home with my body, with myself." For Janice that experience was everything.

The rest of this book unfolds the stories of many others who bring to life the principles and applications of Movement for the Mind and how it can be used to enhance your life.

How to use this Book

The next chapter describes in detail the principles of Movement for the Mind and how it works. Chapter Two walks you through a sample Movement for the Mind session. *The Warm Up and Creative Exploration* sections can be used on their own or to physically warm up the body and refresh your movement vocabulary. Chapters Three through Six discuss four important uses of Movement for the Mind: to reduce our stress levels, to give us greater access to our creativity, and to serve as an effective tool for psychotherapy and physical healing. Each of the chapters concludes with a Movement for the Mind session that you can do in your own home or environment. The final chapter is a compilation of writings by some of the individuals who have experienced this work. They have used their own unique styles to narrate their experiences and to illustrate the dynamic quality that is also available to you.

You can read and do the exercises in order as suggested, or you may read the whole book from beginning to end and then go back and do the exercises that speak most directly to you. You can also use the CD on Movement for the Mind. Either way, it is the experience of this material that will bring the concepts alive for you.

A great teacher of mine once said, "Don't believe the words I tell you. Experience them within yourself. Then you will know the truth."

Through this book I invite you to discover the joy, creativity, and knowledge that lies within you and to rediscover the most natural language of your body, Dance. Dance, not as a specialized art form for the few, but as a soulful, purposeful language for all. Dance that reunites your body with your mind. Dance that awakens your body as a vehicle for guidance and insight, expression, integration and inspiration.

Chapter 1:
What Do you Call This?
Is it Dance?

"Dancing is the loftiest, the most moving,
the most beautiful of the arts, because it is no mere
translation or abstraction from life; it is life itself."
— *Havelock Ellis*

While living in Northern California, I taught a session of a
"Business and Creativity" course that a large and successful private
corporation in Southern California offered to top managers to
increase their motivation and stimulate their creativity. When they
saw the curriculum of the course, several of the executives said,
"If I have to dance in this course I am not taking it under any
circumstances!" The president of the company assured them that no
one would have to "get up and dance in front of everyone."

I flew to Southern California as scheduled and, since I was
going to the airport directly after my session, I brought my overnight
luggage to the class. "I heard there was a rumor circulating that you
might have to dance," I said to the twenty-five participants, most of
them men. "I just want you to know that I have tutus in my bag and
I've brought them in several sizes to fit each one of you!"

That broke the ice. Everyone participated fully, and reported
that they felt more relaxed and had gained new insights that they
could apply both professionally and personally. One male executive
in his sixties practically gushed, "Can we do this every day?" Another
asked me, "What do you call this work? Is it *dance?*"

These executives' responses — their initial resistance and
their later enthusiasm for the work and what it had helped them
accomplish — were neither unusual nor unexpected. As a student in

the Creativity in Business course in the MBA program at Stanford University asked, "What purpose does dance or this movement have? How is this going to improve my creativity or chances in business?" Dance is often regarded as irrelevant for successful, intelligent, motivated adults. It also provokes anxiety.

Why? How have we become so far removed from an activity that is as natural to the body as sounding is to the vocal chords? Why have we become so reliant on the logical mind that we have forgotten the wisdom of the body? How have we kept ourselves separate from our individual artistry and separate from the creative connection to our bodies? How can we place so little value on opportunities that help us increase awareness, consciousness, and healing while we experience a sense of integration and wholeness?

Part of the answer lies in our Western culture. Art became separate from everyday life at the onset of Greek civilization. The concept of a stage was introduced and a symbolic chasm between the "audience" and the "performer" was born. A distinction was made between those who were artists and those who weren't. During the same period, great philosophers such as Socrates and Plato gave the intellect a prominence that still influences us today. Mind and body were made separate, with the mind in the more elevated and significant position. The body was considered secondary.

Religion saw the same segregation. Dancing used to be an important part of all religious rituals. In the Gnostic gospel, *Acts of John*, Jesus was quoted as saying, "To the Universe belongs the dancer." Early Christian congregations performed liturgical dancing until about the seventh century, when dancing was outlawed for being too sensual. The body was allegorically separated from the mind. Dance was taken out of its spiritual context and labeled as secular, base and impure, along with the body.[1]

---

[1] Walker, Barbara R. The Women's Dictionary Of Symbols & Sacred Objects. San Francisco: Harper & Row Publishers, 1988.

Although Eastern mystics associated dancing with Gods and Goddesses such as Shiva and Kali, whose dances expressed the rhythms of life itself, Eastern religious and philosophical traditions also tended to separate body from mind. Even Hatha Yoga (the traditional practice of postures that has become so popular in the West) is practiced largely to purify the body so that the mind can reach ecstatic, altered states of consciousness. Pranayama (powerful breathing techniques) was practiced to achieve out-of-body experiences. The body was viewed as just a shell that could be discarded as easily as a piece of clothing. Being in the body or revering the earth was not viewed as significant; conquering and rising above both was.

Technology has only aggravated our emphasis on the intellect and left-brain. In the twenty-first century, technology has brought us convenience and abundant information. But most of this information needs to be analyzed mentally, and is absorbed as we sit in front of a screen, watch a video, or listen to a lecture. Western culture has honed our intellect and modern technology has created many personal and professional conveniences, but both have also inadvertently contributed to a more fragmented and passive approach to living.

We have become accustomed to having almost everything we need at our fingertips and to accessing knowledge instantly. We are used to swallowing a pill for what ails us physically or emotionally. Yet, there is no magic pill or instant solution to give us creative fulfillment, satisfying intimate relationships, or physical, mental, emotional, and spiritual well-being. These deeper needs require intention, active participation, directed change, conscious integration, and continuous growth and practical application.

As a culture, we have become adept at linear and cognitive thinking, but we have relinquished much of the value placed on imagination, creativity, and active play. However, the challenges that face most of us daily are not just mental and they are not just material.

In her visits to the West, Mother Teresa often commented on the tragic contrast between the material wealth of our population and the emotional and spiritual impoverishment that afflict so many of us.

We have learned to compartmentalize the different aspects of our lives. Separating mind from body, intellect from emotions, and body from spirit, we fragment most of our activities and approach them exclusively rather than inclusively. We exercise our intellects by going to school, we attend to our bodies by working out, we go into therapy to heal our emotions, and we take care of our spiritual needs by attending church or temples of worship. There is no visible integrative link or continuity. In our sophistication, we seem to have lost some of our basic knowledge about how to live.

Feeling the "dis-ease" in our society, many of us today are beginning to pay attention to the practices and philosophies of Native American Indians, Australian Aborigines, and other ancient tribal peoples who understood the delicate balance of life. These cultures used art to express this balance and to honor the interrelatedness between the human body (the individual) and the earth's body (the universal). In valuing their relationship to the earth, they also paid homage to their own creativity. Their bodies and their crafts were an integral part of their heritage and identity.

In most primitive societies including today's Australian Aborigines, dance as an art is not separate from life. The basic life activities — arising, eating, working, courtship and marriage, birthing and dying, healing, making war and peace, enforcing laws — all are ritualized and expressed through dance. Dance is not a separate activity that a few do in their spare time or even an activity that distinguishes the audience from the participant. Dance is a paradigm for life, and through dance the cycles of life are experienced. The body is the instrument for spiritual worship, emotional expression, physical demonstration, and nonverbal communication. In dance, art and life are positively wed, and serve to nurture and sustain the individual and society.

Dance as a creative art activity integrates body, mind, emotions, and spirit. No wonder the Australian Aborigines, American Indians, and countless other cultures incorporated dance as a daily ritual to mirror life's major occurrences. Dance was not just physical exercise, like aerobics, or an elevated art form that few could perform, like ballet, or pure entertainment, like jazz, break or ballroom dancing; it was daily medicine for the body and soul that all people could learn and partake in.

We need to move toward an integrative approach to living; one in which we embrace the physical, mental, emotional, and spiritual components of ourselves and our communities. We need philosophies, activities, and practices that unify these components, not as scattered pieces of a puzzle, but as inseparable colors in a rainbow or octaves on a musical scale.

Movement for the Mind

The technique that I have developed over the past thirty plus years — Movement for the Mind — is such a practice. This technique, which evolved out of the principles of modern dance choreography, dance therapy, and self-awareness techniques such as yoga and guided visualization, has five main stages.

During a session, participants first lie on the floor with their eyes closed and take an "inventory," which is a technique for clearing the mind and becoming more self-aware and conscious of the breath and the physical body. Next, with eyes still closed, participants warm up each part of the body. Then they explore different ways of moving through space. Participants generally move as individuals, but in some sessions they also work and interrelate in groups of two or three. In the fourth stage, participants explore a theme through dance, thus creatively focusing all parts of themselves — body, mind, psyche, and spirit — on one goal. It is this part of the session that is unique to Movement for the Mind. Finally, participants express what they have experienced through another medium such as journaling, drawing or painting, or in a facilitated debriefing session. This final stage integrates intellectual understanding with the physical experience.

People who have participated in Movement for the Mind have reported a wide variety of benefits. Although much of the book will detail these benefits, I'd like to touch upon a few of them now:

- The rewards that come with physical exercise are generated, such as the release of endorphins and the increase of the body's ability to utilize oxygen. A sense of wellness, relaxation, and exuberance accompanies the session.

- Creativity is enhanced. The mind relaxes while the body leads energetically. This can activate insights and realizations that surface freely, bypassing our habitual mental censorship. It can also lead to inspiration in other subjects, art forms and to problem solving.

- Emotions and feelings, including those long forgotten or repressed, can be easily expressed and released.

- Stress is relieved through breathing exercises and other techniques that increase one's control over internal reactions and thus ease the effects of stress.

- Both physical and emotional healing becomes a process of empowerment. Joy and a sense of connection in the body replace the traumas of physical and emotional pain.

- People experience significant psychological breakthroughs and make corresponding positive changes in their daily lives.

These benefits occur through a twofold process. The first part embraces the power of dance itself. The second part addresses the capacity to integrate the power of the mind with the body's intelligence, and speaks to the inherent connection between mind and body.

The rest of this chapter provides the background for understanding why Movement for the Mind is such a powerful path to creative wholeness. First, I discuss the "physical roots" of Movement for the Mind, which include the symbolic nature of dance, and the disciplines of modern dance, and dance therapy. Then I survey what we have learned about the mind/body connection to shed light on why Movement for the Mind can help us lead more fulfilling and satisfying lives.

The Power of Dance

Physically, dance is the creative translation of what we do in this body — move. Dance speaks to every aspect of our being. It challenges us physically and at the same time satisfies the human need for self-expression, communication, and meaning. It demands that the mind be clear, focused, and attentive. Each movement must be birthed from emotional integrity, so that when people dance, they may experience the oneness that mystics speak of reaching in the highest spiritual state. Yogis refer to the creation of the universe as the Dance of Shiva. French author, Anais Nin, coined the phrase "life is a dance," and countless poets and philosophers have made similar analogies between dancing and living.

However, in Western culture dance has been less accessible to the general public than perhaps any other art form. When I was a child, everyone was encouraged to draw and learn to play a musical instrument whether they showed specific artistic talent or not. Although I was offered ballet classes as a child, my brother never took dance lessons. After I stopped taking ballet, I don't remember taking any other class in school that encouraged creative self-expression through the medium of the body.

The purpose of all art is to communicate. Dance communicates through the language of movement. The dancer needs only the body as a vehicle for creative expression. All content comes from the inside and is brought into form through the body. Dancing, singing, and acting are the only art forms that can stand alone without any other embellishments or supportive props. But even the singer and actor need words. Silently, the dancer uses what connects us all to this earth, the body.

In ancient and primitive cultures, symbols and rituals were significant components of everyday life. These cultures, which revered and lived closely with the earth and nature's cycles, utilized movement intentionally as a metaphor for living. They did not rely solely on words to communicate, but understood the power of the symbolic and the power of living in the body. Dance, through its use of gestures, incorporates the symbolic in the acting out of movement. It also allows man to embrace the sacred within his own body.

In the early twentieth century the pioneers of modern dance — including Isadora Duncan, Martha Graham, Ruth St. Denis, and Doris Humphreys — used dance to express once again the passions, pains, and spiritual elements of life. Their dances told stories that contained the emotional and soulful aspects of human experience.

Isadora Duncan understood the power of dance not only to express, but to impact life. She saw dance as the blending of mental and physical discipline, physical agility, emotional content, and soulful expression. Her dance technique, which combined structure with freedom of movement, helped her captivate audiences around the world with her simple but universal gestures. She parlayed in the company of intellectuals, political leaders, and fellow artists. The Russian Revolution colored the times, but Isadora was bent on her own revolution: dance education for all children. She felt that dance could provide a foundation for both the creative and practical lessons of life. Although Isadora's work was cut short by her tragic death, she left a legacy that paved the way for modern dance giant Martha Graham, her contemporaries, and those who followed.

Today the evocative power of movement can still be experienced. For example, at a performance by the Limon Dance Company, the audience was electrified by the dance "Carlota," which is performed without music. The emotions conveyed through silent movement were so forceful that I found myself sitting at the edge of my seat as I absorbed a story of politics and war, love and loss. A second piece, "Heartbeats," wove the cultures and philosophies of more than ten countries. Through music and dance, the choreography brought together these countries' unique flavors and passions. The last section of the dance, "Prayer," made me feel as if I were sitting in an ancient temple. The stage enveloped a sacredness that filled the entire auditorium.

Modern dance pioneers' vision of dance as a universal expression of life is not limited to the relationship between audience and dancer. Without an audience, the process of expressive communication can be an internal experience. The roles of choreographer, audience, and dancer merge into one person. It is this understanding that inspired and led to the work of dance therapists.

Dance therapy, which is primarily a nonverbal, non-tactile process of self-discovery, utilizes the body's movement patterns to communicate, express, and identify whatever that individual is seeking to know. It enables people to let go of the intellect and to allow the creative process to become dominant. Instead of using words, individuals express thoughts, feelings, and experiences through movement. It is distinguished from dance in that dance therapy has no concern for technical skill or outer performance. As in traditional psychotherapy, the dance therapist guides the therapy process for the sole purpose of the participant's self-revelation and healing.

Dance therapy officially began with Marian Chace's work with hospitalized patients and servicemen in the 1940's. At that time there was no term for the experience of post-traumatic stress or for dance therapy. Chace began volunteering at St. Elizabeth's Hospital in Washington D.C. when a hospital administrator invited her to work with a group of patients who were nonverbal and didn't seem to respond to conventional treatment. The administrator thought dance might at least offer them an opportunity for socialization. Chace's work was extremely effective. She was able to establish contact and communication with the patients and to facilitate their healing and recovery. She continued her work for twenty-five more years and was instrumental in training and teaching others about dance therapy. In 1966 she helped found the American Dance Therapy Association (ADTA).

Dance therapists were trained to read a person's body language and to understand movement flow patterns as expressions of specific psychological states. A lot of focus was given to the group process as a source of socialization and using the group format for positive mirroring and interaction. The interaction between dance therapist and patient was also dynamic and included active participation by the therapist.

By the mid-1970s, there were about 500 dance therapists. However, much of the research and fieldwork in dance therapy was limited to a few populations. While Janet Adler did extraordinary work with autistic children; others did clinical work with the mentally retarded and deaf and hospitals conducted dance therapy with chronic and acute schizophrenics. Dance therapy was generally not seen as a full-spectrum therapy, it was viewed as a specialized form that could be effective with disabled populations that did not respond to conventional forms of treatment.

In my experience, dance therapy is not merely an adjunct therapy or form of intervention that should be utilized on a limited basis or as a last resort with problem populations. Dance therapy is a viable and useful technique for most people who are seeking healing, resolution, or simple clarity.

The Movement for the Mind technique I present in this book integrates the symbolic value of dance with the healing legacy of dance therapy, and includes modern dance's vision of authentic expression. It brings back the power of dance to the individual and provides a vehicle for creative self-expression, integration, healing, and for better understanding ourselves and connecting to others.

Connecting the Body and Mind

To understand how Movement for the Mind helps many people make significant changes in their lives, we need to take a closer look at the connection between body and mind. While living in Northern California, I was contacted by the administrator of the Post Traumatic Stress Disorder Clinic at the VA Hospital in Menlo Park, California, to work with women who had been sexually assaulted while serving in the military. The women were in various stages of experiencing trauma including some who were also recalling past memories of child sexual abuse. After conducting a couple of group movement sessions, the administrative and psychiatric staff decided that individual work would be better suited for the population. In one session, a woman was able to recall memories, express and resolve feelings that she had previously negated, and to positively clarify her goals in treatment. After the session the chief psychiatrist said to me, "In a one-hour Movement for the Mind session you've accomplished what would have taken us two years to cover in psychiatry!"

Why was Movement for the Mind so effective? Because body and mind are inextricably linked. The body is affected by the mind, and the body can impact the mind's state.

This insight — that mind and body are one energetic system — is at the heart of the growing field of mind/body medicine and New Age thought. While quantum physicists have confirmed that everything in the universe is composed of energy in the West the connection between mind and body may still seem like a new and trendy idea; yet it is a principle that Eastern forms of philosophy and medicine have incorporated for thousands of years. Inherent in these studies and healing techniques is the understanding that stagnant or blocked energy can lead to physical and psychic breakdown, causing distress and disease.

For example, Chinese medicine states that energy flows through the body through channels called "meridians." In acupuncture, needles are placed at specific points on these meridians to release energy blockages. The energy can then move freely, allowing the surrounding cells and tissues to heal and regenerate.

Eastern forms of movement, including T'ai Chi, Chi Gong, and Yoga, are based on the importance of physical movement for also maintaining the free flow of energy in the body and mind.

In ancient Hindu texts, the energy system of the body is described through the chakras or wheel-like vortexes of energy. These energy centers, located in the spinal cord, are storage centers for knowledge and life experiences. The body, while viewed as temporal, is what holds and carries this information. Whether it is a childhood trauma or a joyous experience, the body stores the memory even when the conscious mind forgets or attempts to block it out.

In the latter part of the twentieth century, researchers shed light on the physical details of how the mind/body connection works. Others have described the same connection from the point of view of people's experiences. I will mention a few of these now and discuss them in greater detail in later chapters.

Scientists in the field of Psychoneuroimmunology (PNI), who have been studying the link between emotions and the body, are finding that the biochemistry of the brain influences every cell in the body, and that these chemicals (neuropeptides) are not only located in the brain or in what we think of as the mind. They have discovered that there are memory cells found throughout the body that create our physical, mental, emotional, and spiritual realities.

Energy medicine practitioners also recognize the influence of thoughts and emotions on the physical body. They view the human body as surrounded by an energy field that is impacted by everything we think, feel, and do. Carolyn Myss, medical intuitive and author of *Anatomy of the Spirit*, has been instrumental in spreading the awareness of energy medicine. She teaches that our biography becomes our biology: our thoughts, actions, and experiences affect our future health. She stresses that imbalances in any aspect of the self — body, mind, emotions, and especially spirit — must be addressed to maintain well-being. She, like many practitioners in this field, believes that holding onto outmoded emotional and behavioral patterns will eventually cause us problems.

Much of this research has centered on acknowledging the power of the mind and its role in healing and maintaining wellness. There are many techniques that stimulate shifts in attitude and awareness; these include psychotherapy, meditation, creative visualization, hypnosis, affirmations, and Neuro Linguistic Programming (NLP). Some of these techniques illuminate the areas where we feel stuck; some concentrate on the desired result. All of them are primarily mental. The body is merely a silent partner in the process.

At the same time, we have seen the development of many techniques for healing and growth that recognize the importance of also engaging the body. Massage therapy, Feldenkrais, Rolfing, Alexander Technique and Heller work, to name a few of the many valid body therapies, evolved out of the recognition of the connection between mind and body. As the body's muscular/skeletal system is manipulated by the practitioner, the client experiences physical shifts that may also impact other areas of his/her life. For example, while being massaged a client may experience an emotional release. In a Feldenkrais session, an individual may find a new way of moving that both releases physical pain and creates a renewed mental state. Yet, while these techniques are very valuable, they must be performed or directed by the practitioner, and primarily focus on the client's physical experience.

Movement for the Mind unites the strengths of these mental techniques, physical disciplines, and bodywork. It resources the body's intelligence and the mind's capacity for creativity and awareness. Because Movement for the Mind stems from dance, its wellspring is art. Dance's ability to evoke, express, and create — which modern dance pioneers understood and dance therapists harnessed — can be achieved by every person who engages in the art of movement with conscious intent.

Intent, or theme, is a key ingredient of Movement for the Mind. In a Movement for the Mind session, it is our intention (or thematic structure) that helps us achieve our goals and provides our sense of meaning. In a dance meant for the stage, the choreographer creates the theme, and the dancer expresses it through movement. In Movement for the Mind, the individual takes on the role of both choreographer and dancer. The theme unfolds through the variation of movement patterns, and we express our intention through these physical actions. In our lives it is also our actions that bring forth our visions into reality. Movement for the Mind helps us experience the movement of our bodies as a microcosm of the larger dance of our lives.

When we explore a theme through movement — whether it is the expression of joy or pain, solving a problem, recalling memories of childhood, understanding the meaning of an illness, feeling more grounded and connected in the body, or simply exploring new ways of moving and feeling — the body experiences a shift that can be felt, repeated, and called upon in a tangible way.

This shift, while it begins in the body, is not necessarily about physical changes; though it can be. The process that unfolds for every person is that they connect with something basic within themselves. One individual may change her movement style by walking or holding her posture differently. Another person may lose weight. A third may change his behavioral patterns and how he interacts with others. It is not so much about being able to move in a new way as it is about moving in order to stimulate new states of awareness, which then catalyze the appropriate changes for each individual.

Conscious intent coupled with movement can be applied to virtually any goal. Researchers have discovered that the more senses we can engage in an activity, the more actual and present we can make a desired goal; the easier it can manifest. It does not seem to matter whether the desired result is the healing of cancer, chronic pain, an emotional trauma, or whether it is the desire to change jobs or find a more suitable vocation. Part of the reason Movement for the Mind is so effective is that it employs all of the body's senses to bring about the desired result.

In a Movement for the Mind session, a participant experiences the power of the body/mind connection both passively (unconsciously) and actively (consciously). In the first part of the dance session, breath, mental imagery, music, and the exploration of emotions call upon and integrate body, mind, psyche, and spirit. In the next step, the use of a theme is like a laser beam that directs the energy toward the desired outcome, and drives this unconscious integration to a conscious place.

For example, someone with cancer may get in touch with feelings of tightness and realize that she has been living with this knot for as long as she can remember. For another, images of never being able to express his needs as a child may surface. In Movement for the Mind sessions, people learn how to express these feelings and to release the tightness resulting from emotional constriction. They begin to let go of old mental and emotional states and to move differently in their bodies. (The difference may or may not be perceptible to anyone else.) They then replace old constructs with new thoughts and behaviors.

Movement that is engaged consciously can anchor the new belief. When we apply the principles of body/mind connection, energy medicine, and the science of Psychoneuroimmunology, we begin to grasp the synergy and life force in the body. The more aware we become in the body, the more control we can have over our health, mental state, and happiness.

So while we may intellectually know that our bodies and minds are connected, Movement for the Mind can help us use this connection. In the past thirty years, I have watched with awe as private clients and participants in workshops and group sessions have harnessed the power of dance — to achieve greater knowledge of themselves, to experience catharsis through the expression and release of memories and emotions, to give them clarity and calm in the midst of chaos, and to achieve a sense of joy and oneness with their bodies, emotions, and spirits. I invite you to join them.

Chapter 2:
The Practice of Moving Mindfully

"I see the dance being used as a
means of communication between soul and soul —
to express what is too deep, too fine for words."
— *Ruth St. Denis*

In this chapter we will look at the principles and dynamics that make up a Movement for the Mind session. In the first part of the session, you will learn self-awareness tools to open the breath and calm the mind. Then you will warm up the physical body and explore movement vocabulary as a way to engage your body creatively. The second part of this session integrates a theme with the movement technique that you have just learned.

The technique can be experienced in a group or alone. The first part of the session always focuses on you, the individual. In the thematic portion, interrelating with others can encourage communication, relationship, and team building skills. In the following pages, I describe the creative process from the perspective of participating in a group. However, you can do the exercise at the end of the chapter alone or with others. Let's begin the journey.

The Practice

The movement vocabulary that I have developed is based on five dance choreographic principles: time, space, energy, rhythm, and motion. Music is an important component as it lends emotional and environmental content. For example, using music that is melodious and harmonious can create a calming mood and a peaceful environment, whereas dissonant tones may arouse agitation and its opposite ambiance. In most dance or movement classes, the students follow the teacher's direction, copying the moves and learning specific steps and choreographed movements. Movement for the Mind sessions are verbally guided and are not based on technical skill. There are no precise movements to copy or follow.

There is no audience, so each participant becomes both the audience and the performer. Instead of telling a story to an audience, an inner drama is expressed. It is a dance for the inner self. This is dance in its purest form, for it embraces what is essential in us. It is not for show, but for sustenance. It is not for outer applause or approval, but for self-exploration and for expressing the calls of life. Foremost, it is a tool for knowledge. There is no right or wrong way to move and the pace is always self-regulated.

Self-Awareness

The initial process is inner-directed, and heightens participants' awareness of feeling safe and grounded in the body. Taking off their shoes, participants leave their "voice of judgment" with their shoes. This is the internal critic that tells us that "we're not good enough; we can't do this" and often sabotages and prevents us from fully exploring our creativity.

Breathing

Lying on the floor comfortably with the eyes closed, participants first focus on their breathing. Learning how to breathe properly by slowing the breath down and filling the diaphragm and lungs more fully is an essential ingredient to staying connected in the body. There are many books about the science of breath. The ancient Yogis, as well as masters in other cultures, understood the power of the breath. The complete breath technique I teach, activates awareness of the breath in the torso and also emphasizes the exhalation.

Breathing through the nostrils, participants begin by inhaling from the lower belly, slowly bringing the breath into the outer edges of the diaphragm, filling the ribs fully, and then finally raising the breath into the chest. Once we have inhaled maximally without struggling, the exhalation begins slowly and deeply out through the nostrils until the breath is fully released. In this complete breath, it is not necessary to hold the breath between inhalations and exhalations. The emphasis is on fullness, gently activating as much of the torso as possible in each section of the breath, and on the complete release of the exhalation. In our modern Western culture, metaphorically speaking, we ingest far more then we tend to let go. For many, the awareness of releasing is as important as filling up.

Boundaries

Still with the eyes closed, participants then explore a technique for identifying appropriate boundaries in the body. Creating appropriate boundaries is something few of us were taught as children. Some of us have built unconscious energetic walls as boundaries to protect ourselves, while others are more invasive and need constant contact and acknowledgment. Connecting in the body and realizing and maintaining appropriate boundaries is key to a healthy relationship with ourselves and with others.

The skin is used to identify our physical boundaries. By focusing on feeling the skin's texture along the surface of the body, participants differentiate their physical body from the floor, air, music, my voice, and everything else around them. As children, many of us learned to split or disassociate from the body when we felt scared or threatened. Becoming aware of the skin serves to define our physical boundaries and to reaffirm a sensation of grounding and being fully present in the body.

Once participants define their physical boundaries, they can establish inner boundaries. Individuals sense any restrictions in the body and mentally expand the space inside the skin until there is a feeling of safety, freedom, comfort, and sanctity. Our inner boundaries define what is inwardly personal and can comfortably house our feelings, memories, and visions. Consciously establishing outer and inner boundaries allows us to appropriately stand our ground while being open and compassionate with others without having to be defensive.

Inventory

Subsequently, participants take a physical, mental, emotional, and spiritual inventory. Most of us are so busy just keeping up with our fast-paced lives that we tend to operate on automatic pilot. We rarely take the time to observe what we are thinking or feeling. It is precisely this state of being out of touch with what is occurring within us that leads to panic when we get sick or when we are faced with emotional states that we don't know how to handle. By taking the time to replace unconscious thoughts and actions with awareness, we can make better choices and even interrupt negative thought patterns before they lead to undesirable actions.

Movement Vocabulary

The Warm Up

The next step is to begin moving the different parts of the body. We use the body as an instrument, and warming it up is as essential as doing scales on the piano. This stage is designed to encourage exploration, develop a movement vocabulary, and promote a sense of safety and comfort in the body. For many of us it is like learning a new language.

Yet, movement is the most natural thing we do. Babies move their tiny limbs effortlessly. They stretch and wiggle, and when they begin to crawl and eventually walk, we applaud every new movement. But most of us, as we enter adulthood, censor what once came naturally and spontaneously. We limit our movements to what is conventional. We walk, exercise, engage in sports, but how many of us walk backwards, sideways, or turning? When do we just explore walking, running, crawling, jumping, sliding, or skipping for the sheer joy of moving? How many of us, left to our own devices, would break out carving shapes in space the way many people start humming or speaking aloud?

As participants move each part of the body, they begin to really feel their bodies perhaps for the first time. They move torso, joints, limbs, and muscles, first in isolation and then in harmony, until they are synchronized like instruments in an orchestra. The rhythm of the breath accompanies the continuous flow of moving limbs, and then participants experiment with movements that pause, stop and begin again, called interrupted flow. We then add changing levels from lying on the floor (low level) to sitting and kneeling (middle level), and finally standing (high level). As we come to standing level, the feet, legs, and lower torso become the focal point. The feet are planted firmly against the floor like giant roots, while participants explore the sturdiness of the legs and the power center at the navel.

We call the bottom of the feet, "soles." ("Souls" of the feet.) When we move, the feet are what connect us to the earth. Yet, few of the individuals in the yoga, fitness, and movement sessions I've taught had been taught to pay attention to their feet. In Yogic tradition, the awakened energy and power of the great masters or Gurus emanates most strongly from their feet. It is the ultimate blessing to touch or come into contact with the Guru's feet.

In T'ai Chi and other Eastern forms of exercise, all movement is generated from the chi or power center around the navel. Moving from this center establishes a focal point and is essential to all other movements.

Working in private Movement for the Mind sessions with individuals who felt powerless in different areas of their lives, I have found that grounding and establishing this contact with the feet and with the power center around the navel has a strong influence. After several sessions of reclaiming the energetic connection to their feet, legs, hips, and pelvis, they begin not only to move differently in their bodies, but also to experience taking action in their lives with more confidence, clarity, purpose, and assurance. This shift in the body allows them to feel more grounded and connected in their world.

When the experience of being grounded has been established, participants shift their weight forward, backward, and side to side to challenge their balance. With their eyes closed, students stand on one leg, balance on one hand and knee, lean to the right, lean to the left, and begin to take tiny steps out into the room. They judge their boundaries with a kinesthetic sense, feeling the energy around them rather than using their sense of sight.

Exploration

Finally, it is time to move throughout the room on low, middle, and high levels using forward, backward, sideways, and turning motions. Low level is defined by keeping all of our body parts on the floor as in lying down, middle level is when we sit, kneel, or crawl, and high level includes all movements that we do while standing on or moving off the floor as in jumping or leaping. Participants open their eyes for physical safety, but the focus is still inward. The exploration now expands into new movement vocabulary and sequences. Since life is filled with polarities, using polarities in movement can be quite expansive and instructional. Moving on any level while changing directions, participants begin to explore angular, bound, heavy, and direct movements. Then they discover the opposite dynamics: curved shapes, free, light, and indirect movements. These flow patterns, taken from Laban Movement Analysis, were originally developed by Rudolph Laban and Warren Lamb in the early 1900's to identify different movement behavioral patterns and to describe their correlating psychological connection. The addition of various tempos from slow to fast and even and uneven rhythms creates a potpourri of choices. Participants experience themselves larger than life and smaller than invisible, both emotional and visual responses occur spontaneously while moving.

Participants learn a lot just by witnessing the simplicity of these movements. The exploration is physical, but they begin to assess certain movements as comfortable, some as foreign, and others as surprisingly refreshing. Most of us are locked into repetitive and sometimes limited behavioral patterns that can be translated into movement. Individuals who deliberate between sentences, plan concisely before taking action and are perfectionists will choose shapes and movements that mimic that behavior. Exploring the opposite movement dynamics allows participants to experience themselves differently.

For example, one student, a towering presence at six feet five inches, exclaimed, "The only way I've known how to move is bound and strong. I loved moving light and fluffy. It actually felt more comfortable and less constraining. I didn't even know that sensation was available to me!"

By using these different movement dynamics, participants develop a varied movement vocabulary that allow them to begin exploring personal themes. Each one of us has a unique movement style. The many facets of our personality and psyche are determined in part by the events in our past, by what motivates us, by the expectations of others, and by how we view ourselves; they are expressed through our movements.

Themes — Adding Conscious Intention

Having explored the full range of movement dynamics, participants explore a theme after the warm up and exploration. It is this part of the session that extends our possibilities into the extraordinary. The theme provides the participant with a conscious intention and this is what feeds the creative process and transforms ordinary physical movement into the potential for healing physical and emotional trauma, shifting behavior, finding solutions to problems, and dynamically creating new choices. Conscious intention is the energetic bridge between the mind and body.

Using high, middle, and low levels, forward, backward, sideways and turning motions, fast and slow tempos, even and uneven rhythms, and large and small shapes, participants begin to explore their own distinct movement styles. Instead of wearing a name tag to identify who they are, they dance their name tag. Leading with different parts of the body, using direct or indirect movements, angular or curved shapes, bound or free, and weak or strong energetic motions, they begin to identify patterns of movement that most comfortably communicate how they see themselves.

Still moving, participants now contemplate where they might like to be in their lives five years from now. They begin to project their goals into the future through their movements and focus on the attributes it would require of them.

Using the movement vocabulary they have just explored and new mental images, they add movements to reflect these changes. For example, a participant who wants to change her career from working for a large corporation to becoming an entrepreneur may use movements that are both expansive and yet focused and direct. Free and uneven rhythms may replace the bound and even motions of her earlier dance.

Personal goals can also be explored. A single participant may begin moving as if he is part of a family. His movements may become larger, and he may add curved, flexible shapes and indirect motions to reflect these lifestyle changes. The kinesthetic feelings are as important as the physical movements. Participants use their own mental and emotional imagery as well as physical movement patterns to weave their goals. Participants may discover movements that they never would have previously explored such as moving from place to place on the floor on their backs. Feelings of support and yet freedom issuing from these movements may inspire them to a different experience of themselves. They learn how to trust their bodies to guide them.

Themes for groups

Even in a group setting, the emphasis is on the individual. However, since dance is ultimately about communication the creative process can also include exploring this component with others.

In our personal and work lives, communicating effectively is essential. For the most part in our society, we rely on words to express our thoughts, feelings, and actions. Yet, many of us mask the truth with words. Body language may actually signal the opposite of what our words are saying. As modern dance pioneer Agnes De Mille said, "Bodies never lie."

Using dance, groups of two or three can be formed specifically to work on communication skills. After the warm up and exploration section, two or three individuals find themselves face to face. Now they must connect and relate to someone else without giving up their own movements. Since all these decisions and communications must occur non-verbally, subtleties are noticed. After their initial connection, I instruct each small group to shift their relationship dynamic and to begin to mirror each other. They decide non-verbally who will lead and who will follow, and then the roles are reversed.

Next, I ask them to explore conversations where the movements flow back and forth between them spontaneously. All the while, I coach the participants to retain their boundaries and notice how they can be in relationship without sacrificing their own movements. This is not an easy task even with words.

Eventually each group is asked to move as one unit. Outwardly they are mirroring each other, changing movements and leaders continuously. Inwardly they are asked to stay cognizant of their own styles and boundaries.

From this point, the session can go in several different directions. The participants can change partners, repeating the same process in the new partnership, or they can separate and go back to their movements as individuals. In sessions specifically set up to deal with relationship issues, I introduce several other dynamics that simulate conflict resolution and offer communication tools from varying psychological perspectives. For example, we may look at how a participant reacts while he experiences being emotionally attacked or pressured and how he can communicate those feelings without becoming defensive or withdrawing.

Dancing in dyads or triads can lead to powerful insights. One manager in a corporate Business and Creativity course shared, "I always thought I was a very expressive person until you took our words away from us. I actually froze for a few minutes. This whole experience is something new for me." A therapist in a course designed for Marriage, Family, Child Counseling Certificate candidates (MFCC), learned compassion for another individual's point of view where she normally would have resorted to judgment and resistance. Another course participant said, "I didn't realize how difficult it is to maintain my own boundaries. I find myself always trying to please others and do the right thing, so following was easier for me than leading." While someone else overcame her shyness and uncharacteristically enjoyed relating to people she didn't know.

The purpose of these insights is to enable individuals to understand and clarify their motivations and actions, and expand their choices. Most of us act out behavioral patterns that we sculpted in childhood. Some of these patterns benefit us, but many are antiquated and are acted out by rote. The more awareness we each cultivate, the more tolerance we can have for ourselves and those around us. The goal of group work is to enrich our relationships and create greater clarity and integrity in our communications.

Practice Closure

The dance session is brought to a close after the theme is fully explored. This process began with the eyes closed, *complete breath,* and an inventory that connects the individual to the inner dynamics of body, mind, emotions, and spirit. The session ends by returning full circle to this initial awareness. Participants are asked to still their outer movements while continuing to pay attention to the inner rhythm of their breath. They may remain standing or choose to lie down or take a sitting posture. They close their eyes and turn their attention inward. Connecting to their boundaries, they repeat the inventory taken at the beginning of the practice. As participants turn their attention to the physical, mental, emotional and spiritual components, they mentally note shifts that have taken place so that they can be discussed or written down for further insight. Participants are asked to gently open their eyes and regroup by sitting in a circle for the final portion of the session.

For some this is the most difficult part of the session. After having been nonverbal for an hour or longer, articulating the experience into words and sharing that experience can be challenging. It is ironic, since so many of us are hardly ever at a loss for words. As much as we overly rely on words to communicate, I also feel that verbally relating our experiences and observations or writing them down if you are doing the session on your own helps to consciously build the bridge between the intellect and the body. By articulating the perceptive changes that have occurred, the different sensations in the body, and the emotional and mental insights, we clarify the experience and make it real. The sensations and shifts did not just occur in some dream state or as a figment of our imagination. They were felt, moved, and then spoken or written about. So the experience becomes tangible on every level. The more tangible we can make any experience, the more easily we can repeat it and translate it into our daily lives.

Sharing the experience verbally also helps confirm our diversity and our sense of connectedness. Some experiences are universal and others are individual. One person might discover a sense of freedom and joy that carries forward from the warm up to the end of the session. A man in his mid-twenties from the Middle East shared, "In the last section while lying on the floor observing my body, I noticed that I felt tingly, warm, full of energy, and yet I was totally relaxed. My mind was quiet, which is amazing. I loved learning this way, but in the beginning I was apprehensive, as I had never experienced anything like this before in my culture." Others nodded their heads in agreement. Someone else saw the same exercise completely differently, finding value in an opposite sensation.

There is no right or wrong way to move or right or wrong way to feel, and realizing that truth is an essential component of Movement for the Mind. Whenever we explore new territories, whether it is a physical or a mental journey, it is important to feel safe and supported in the validity of our experience. It is the impact of the experience translated into form that brings it to life and ultimately allows it to be integrated positively into our lives.

In the movement vocabulary exercise that follows, you will experience the first stage of a Movement for the Mind session, including awakening awareness in the body, the Warm Up, Creative Exploration, and working with personal themes. First read the Dance Principles section several times to become more familiar with the vocabulary used in the session. Repeat the session as often as you like, and keep a journal to jot down feelings, insights, and any other

sensations you experience after each session. You may also want
to read the instructions several times so that you are familiar with
each section before doing it. Or you can read the instructions into a
recording device and then let your own voice instruct you. You can
also use the CD, "Movement for the Mind," to guide your session.

Using dance in this way will be a unique experience. Be
willing to treat each session as if it were brand new. You may have a
profound experience. You may feel nothing. Allow the practice of
moving to be enough. Begin to have more and more reverence for
the inherent creativity of your body, for the pulsation and depth
of your breath, and for the awareness you are beginning to bring
to your mental, emotional, physical and spiritual states. Be willing
to trust the inherent intelligence of your body. Each subsequent
chapter will unfold another aspect of using Movement for the Mind
to explore new information.

Dance Principles

Dance Principles are the origin of all choreography, be it a ballet
classic, a modern piece, a jazz review, or an individual's expression
of feelings. They are the modality to express all facets of the body's
language. They are the tools that bring the body to life as an
instrument of expression and communication.

Dance Principles are: Time, Space, Energy, Motion and Rhythm.

Time identifies the duration and speed at which we move.
Some people move like bullets - always dashing - some people
move slowly and deliberately. Learning to vary speed creates new
possibilities. They are:

• Fast

• Slow

• Short duration

- Long duration

- Variations between the extremes of speed and duration.

Space identifies our relationship of our body to itself, to its environment, and to others. It depicts our boundaries. Shapes are created through varying *levels,* which are used to measure spatial patterns. We speak of "carving" space by creating movements with our body parts in relationship to the body and to the immediate environment. We use *isolated* movements to carve our shapes in place and *locomotor* movements to delineate space from place to place. The *Levels* are:

- Low — We keep all of our body parts in contact with the floor by lying down.

- Middle — We sit, kneel, or crawl.

- High — Includes all movements that we do while standing with our feet in contact with the floor, and when we move off the floor to jump, leap, or run.

Energy portrays how we move in space; it delineates quality of movement and flow. Energy is most closely related to emotion and creates variation and mood changes. Using opposite flows of energy generates a wide range of compositional possibilities and emotional exploration. Some polarities of energy are:

- Bound/Free

- Staccato/Smooth

- Continuous/Interrupted

- Explosive/Implosive

- Loud/Quiet

- Strong/Weak

- Big/Small

- Heavy/Light

- Angular/Curved

Motion is the movement we actually generate. It delineates path and direction. In motion we integrate time, space, and energy. We can move forward, backward, sideways or turning. We can move in straight, curved, zig zag, or diagonal paths. Motion can be vertical or horizontal and uses all the planes of the body. Motion can be *isolated* or *locomotor*. In *isolated* movement we move the parts individually, orchestrating and integrating the parts of the body without actually traveling in space. *Locomotor* movement is what creates our motion from place to place. *Locomotor* movement consists of the following:

- Walking

- Running

- Jumping

- Leaping

- Skipping

- Galloping

- Sliding

- Crawling

Rhythm is most closely related to the breath. It is characterized by a beat or pulse and is the music of the body. It can be expressed in even or uneven beats. It is the core of all composition. Rhythm creates the underlying theme and pattern to movement and offers continuity and change to whatever is expressed.

When integrated together, *Dance Principles* can create infinite variations that allow the individual to not only express the Self but to alter recurring or self-limiting patterns of movement. In understanding and using *Dance Principles*, we are offered choices to vary our movement, to expand our possibilities, and to experience many new avenues of relating and moving in our bodies in creative and self-expressive ways.

Exercise: Developing a Movement Vocabulary

The following exercise is to be used to awaken awareness in the body, to create agility, and as your movement "technique" and structure for exploring a theme. You can practice the entire session alone or use the first three sections, skipping the personal themes part, as a warm up for the exercises at the end of Chapters Three through Six. The more that you practice this exercise, the more comfortable you will become using your body as a creative vehicle for many different types of movement.

For example, one Movement for the Mind client participated in a yoga workshop that I gave. She did all of the postures with ease and flow and it seemed like she had been practicing yoga for years. When I asked her about this, she said, "Actually this is the first time I've ever done yoga. I don't do any formal exercise, except I do practice the *Movement for the Mind* CD three to four times a week to relieve stress and to keep my body supple."

I also recommend using the breathing exercise described in this session on its own whenever you are under stress or in need of extra energy. It can help you feel more grounded and alive in the body. An easy schedule would be to practice the *complete breath* for five minutes in the morning and five minutes before you go to sleep at night.

Before you begin the session, survey your room and make sure you have the privacy and space that you need without bumping into anything. Any room will do as long as you can stretch out and take several large steps in all directions. Take off your shoes, place them out of your way, and then leave your voice of judgment — the internal critic that might label or judge your movements or feelings — with your shoes.

After you have completed the exercises, write down the feelings, sensations, or any other impulses that you may have experienced while moving. The most important point is to let your body do the communicating and to not judge or censor any of the movements or feelings.

Remember to read the entire section through once and then you may want to record the instructions on tape and move to the sound of your own voice pausing in the appropriate places to give yourself time to complete each task.

Musical Selections: Feel free to add music to your sessions. Music is a motivator, it can support the environment that you are creating or it can work against it like a distraction. Whatever you choose, make sure you stay aware of your reactions and your boundaries. There will be four sections in this session. Make sure that the CD's are easily accessible so that there is minimal distraction when you change the music. Or you can pre-select your music on your I-Pod or any other electronic device. Stay connected to your feelings as you change the music. For the Warm Up choose a piece of music that flows. You can use any piano music or instrumental that is harmonious and calming, yet is upbeat enough to keep you moving. I suggest Yanni's, *In My Time* or *Coming Home* by Andy Bryner. For the second section, choose music that is energetic and has a good beat to it. *Dancing On The Planet* is a good choice. For the last section use any piece that makes you feel good. It can be peaceful or upbeat. You can use the same music you danced to in the Warm Up.

Section I: Self-Awareness

Breathing

Find a spot in the room that you feel comfortable in and have the physical dimensions to move in all directions without bumping into anything. Lie down on your back with your feet straight in front of you and your arms comfortably by your side. Close your eyes. You will keep your eyes closed until we begin the Creative Exploration section. (About fifteen minutes.) If you wear contacts and it is uncomfortable to keep your eyes closed for an extended time, please take them out. It is important for you to be physically comfortable while journeying inward.

Begin by first just observing your breath. Notice where you feel the movement in your body and if you are breathing through your mouth or your nostrils. I'm going to teach you the *complete breath* in stages and will ask you to breathe through the nostrils throughout the exercise. If you find it difficult to breathe this way, do the best you can without straining. It will become easier with practice.

First put your hands on the lower part of your abdomen. Take three breaths filling your belly like a balloon. Don't let your chest or diaphragm get activated, just your belly. After three breaths relax your breathing and move your hands up to both sides of your ribs. (Pause) Now, expand your rib cage and your diaphragm like an accordion, isolating the breath in just this area. The lower abdomen will remain unaffected while your diaphragm moves and expands sideways. Do this three times and then again return to your natural breath. (Pause) Finally, move your hands to the chest area stacking them palm down on top of each other. Isolate your breath in the upper chest. You may feel a very subtle forward and backward motion under where your hands are stacked. Also do this three times and then relax your hands back to your side comfortably and breathe normally. (Pause)

Now you are going to put these three stages together as you inhale. First bring the breath up filling the belly, then gently move your breath to the diaphragm, and finally bring it up to your chest. You may pause for a moment and then slowly exhale. Your exhalation should be at least twice as long as your inhalation. Then when you have completely emptied the breath begin the inhalation again. Do the whole series for at least five rounds. Remember to not struggle. It is important to completely exhale the breath before you take in the next inhalation. Execute the inhalation as smoothly as you can. You may not be able to breathe very deeply at first, but with practice your breath will get slower, deeper, and longer. (Pause)

After the fifth round allow the natural rhythm of your breath to return. Just observe the natural rhythm of your breath for another five rounds. Allow this natural flow of the in breath and the out breath to be the gauge for the rhythm in your movement patterns.

Boundaries

Become aware of your physical boundaries. You will define your physical boundaries through the skin on the surface of your body, which differentiates you from the floor, the air, the music, and even the instructions in this section. Touch your skin with your hands so that you know where your body's surface begins and ends. Make sure there is no place on your skin that is numb or undefined where you can disassociate from your body. If there is, use your hands to feel the skin there and to remind you to stay inside your boundaries. Take as long as you need to identify your outer boundaries thoroughly. (Pause)

Once you have defined your physical boundaries, mentally go inside your skin and make the space on the inside as spacious and secure as you can conceive. There should be no feelings of restriction here. These are your inner boundaries. It is on the inside that you can safely house your memories, feelings, dreams, images, and inner child. No one can judge, change, or invalidate this place within your outer boundaries.

Physical, mental, emotional, and spiritual inventory

Now be aware of your physical body. Notice any heat or cold, comfort or discomfort. Be aware of your energy level. Do you feel tired or invigorated? Do not feel like you have to change anything. Just observe your physical body without judgment for thirty seconds to a minute. Change your focus to your mental state. Is your mind quiet or full of chatter? What is the quality of your thoughts? Simply observe your mental state for about thirty seconds. Now check in with your emotional state. What feelings are available to you right now? Sadness? Joy? Anger? Numbness? Neutrality? Without judging, just notice what you feel. Last but not least become aware of what I call the witness. It is the part of you that no matter what you have gone through is always OK. It is the knower in you who remembers your dreams. You may also call this part source, spirit, or soul. Locate the witness somewhere in your physical body. You may find it in your heart, solar plexus, or anywhere else.

Section II: Warm Up

Low Level

You are now going to begin moving and warming up the body while lying on the floor in low level. Let your body be completely supported by the floor. Imagine that you have just been given this body and that you are going to explore how it moves and communicates for the very first time, isolating one body part at a time. You will begin with the feet. Moving the feet, notice what stretches. How many feet do you have? Are they connected? Notice the toes, arches, and metatarsals. Can feet fly, wiggle, stomp? In 1989, Daniel Day Lewis won the academy award for best performance in the film, "My Left Foot." He portrayed the story of a man who was paralyzed in every part of his body except his left foot. This man became a world class artist who used his foot to hold the paint brush and paint. What would you communicate to the world with just your feet?

Now add your ankles and legs to your movements. Notice that you have knees, thighs and joints. Feet, ankles, and legs moving now. Do they move separately or together? How much more freedom do you have moving these parts of your body? We will now add a movement flow. Move continuously so that one movement flows into the next without pausing or stopping. You may move at any tempo but don't stop. Notice if this is comfortable or uncomfortable without judging yourself.

Gently let your movements come to a stillness and just see if you feel any difference in the lower part of your body from the rest of you. Still lying on the floor in low level, begin moving your head, neck, and face. How far does your neck rotate? Notice what feels expansive and what feels like a limitation. Move parts of your face including your mouth, eyes, brow, and nose. Do your ears move? How does this part of your body differ from your feet and legs? What feels the same? Now continue moving adding your shoulders, arms, wrists, and fingers.

While moving these body parts, change your flow pattern to interrupted movement. Instead of allowing your movements to be continuous, stop and pause, then begin again. Notice if this feels more or less comfortable then the continuous flow pattern. How do your arms connect to your neck, hands, and fingers? Punch, float, wiggle, and rotate these parts. Why do we associate touch with the hands and fingers? Is the touch soft or rough? Continue moving a few more minutes. (Pause) Then bring your movements to a closure.

Now you will move the torso. Feel your ribs, waist, abdomen, hips, and buttocks. Let go of the interrupted flow pattern and now continue varying your flow between both continuous and

interrupted movements. Experiment with either flow for as long
or as short a duration as you like. How does the center of your
body move? Extend your ribs forward, backward, and side-to-side.
Then do the same with your hips. Feel your belly full of breath than
contract your stomach. How would you communicate with the world
if only these parts of your body moved? (Pause) Again gently let
your movements come to a stillness.

Middle Level

Up to now you have been moving only on low level. Next, move
from low level to middle level. Middle level takes your body up to
sitting or kneeling. You will begin to take weight on different parts of
the body working against the pull of gravity. In addition to moving
up to middle level, begin orchestrating the different parts of your
body together. Using both continuous and interrupted flows, move
your upper body with your lower body. Create different combinations:
moving the arms with your feet, head with your hips, legs with your
shoulders, and so on. Do these different combinations on both low
and middle levels. Notice the difference between having your body
completely supported on the floor in low level and having to support
yourself by placing your weight on different body parts in middle
level. Take weight on your hands and knees, then support yourself
on your buttocks and feet. Try different combinations. Continue your
exploration in low and middle levels for another few minutes. (Pause)

High level

Still moving, come up to high level taking the weight onto your
feet. However, the first time you come up to high level, give into the
pull of gravity and come right back to the floor. Do this gently of
course, still with your eyes closed. The next time you come up to
your feet, imagine that there is rubber cement glue on the soles of
your feet and that your feet stick to the floor wherever you stand up.
Your feet may be turned in or out and your stance may be narrow or

wide. If you come up in an awkward position, adjust your feet and then ground them to the floor. Keep moving the different parts of your body above your feet.

Grounding

Feel your feet actually becoming wider and longer, supporting your body with strength and certainty. Imagine that your feet are growing roots connecting the soles of your feet from the floor to the center of the earth. Still moving above the feet, bring your attention to your legs and hips. Allow the energy and support that you are beginning to generate in your feet to travel up your legs to the area around your navel. Feel the power and strength in your lower abdomen, hips, legs, and feet. Continue moving above the feet while focusing and generating energy in the lower part of your body for a few more minutes. (Pause)

On and Off Balance

Still with your eyes closed, mentally remove the rubber cement from the soles of your feet and begin taking steps forward, backward, and sideways. Then experiment by altering how you place your weight on your feet. Take your weight onto your toes leaning forward, lean back on your heels, and then move side to side on your feet. How far can you go without falling over? Now play with your balance. Stand on one leg, then the other. Stretch out to the left and then to the right. How else can you test your balance? Stay with this for a few more minutes. (Pause)

Section III: Creative Exploration

You're now going to begin moving out into the room. Gently open your eyes focusing on the floor so that your attention is still inward and not distracted by your environment or anything else as you begin locomoting around the room. You may walk, run, jump, gallop, crawl, skip, slide, or hop depending upon the amount of space you have. Use all three levels: low, middle, and high. You can move in four directions: forward, backward, sideways, and turning. You have two flow patterns: continuous and interrupted, and you can use all parts of your body to generate and motivate your motion. (Pause)

Now, begin doing bound, strong, direct, and angular movements. It can be at any level, in any direction with any flow pattern. Notice how you feel when you move this way. Is it familiar or unfamiliar? Continue moving with bound, strong, direct, and angular movements and add the tempo, fast. Move faster... faster... faster. Remember you are still exploring bound, strong, direct, and angular movements. Now slow your movements down. Slower. Outer space slow. Continue moving. (Pause)

Instead of bound, move free, light, indirect, and use curved shapes. Continue moving slowly while exploring these qualities. (Pause) Are you more comfortable using these patterns? Are they familiar? Still moving free, light, indirect, and curved change your tempo to fast. Can you still maintain the integrity of your movements while moving fast? Faster... Lighter... Freer... (Pause)

Let go of these qualities and physically doodle with all these movement choices. You have low, middle, and high levels. You can move forward, backward, sideways, and turning. You can move continuously or with pauses. You can go fast or slow. You can move bound or free, strong or light, direct or indirect, and you can create curved or angular shapes. Try different combinations together. Let your movements be motivated by different body parts. Lead with your left side. (Pause) Lead with your buttocks. (Pause) Lead with your head. (Pause) Change levels. (Pause)

Continue moving but make all your movements big. Imagine that your body is ten feet tall and ten feet wide. Feel that your movements take over the room. Everything about you is visible, powerful, and noticeable. Does this make you feel comfortable or uncomfortable? (Pause) Now do the opposite. Your body has become Lilliputian. Everything including your movement gestures are small, even tiny. If you ever felt like disappearing into the cracks of the floor, this is the time. How does it feel to move as if you were imperceptible? (Pause)

Release these "small" gestures and continue doodling. Move in even rhythms. Notice if the music supports your maintaining an even rhythm or compels you to syncopation. Stay with all even motions. Fast or slow, big or small, on any level, in any direction. (Pause) Now change your movements to reflect uneven rhythms. Which feels more challenging? Which feels more natural to your own body's innate rhythm? Which more closely resembles your breath? (Pause)

Let go of this specific exploration of even and uneven rhythms and add it to your vocabulary. Work with all the different elements that you have explored in the Warm Up and in this section. Continue moving another few minutes. (Pause)

Section IV: Personal Themes

Out of the exploration you have just experienced, create a dance that personifies who you are. Dance a name tag for yourself. Express how you see yourself. How you think you come across in the world, including your personality traits, strengths, and weaknesses. Are you strong, bound, and direct? Which flow pattern do you use predominantly? Do you pause before speaking your mind? Do you tend to talk and move quickly? Would you describe yourself as someone who is motivated by your intellect or by your passions? Do you command a room when you walk in or do you remain largely invisible observing details from the sidelines? Without judging yourself, begin to physically and energetically express the many facets of who you are through the language of the body you have just learned in the Warm Up and Creative Exploration sections. Do not strain mentally. Let your body do the talking. (Pause) Continue unfolding this dance for another five to seven minutes.

Still moving, contemplate where you might like to be in your life five years from now. If five years feels too far away, change the timing to three years from now. Think about the traits and qualities you still want to develop, the lifestyle, and professional goals you may want to achieve. Choose one or two areas and focus on the attributes it would require of you.

For example if you want to go back to school, it would require patience, discipline, and focus. If you are single and would like to have more love in your life, what would it feel like in your body to be in that relationship? Would you move more slowly with curved shapes? Let your thoughts entertain the future and then begin to moderate your movements to include the embodiment of these goals. If you are satisfied with your life as it is in the present, what qualities could you further develop? Life always calls us to growth. What do you aspire to?

Use the movement material in the name tag theme that you have just experienced. Do these changes reflect even or uneven rhythms? Do you need to add movements that hug the floor assuring you grounding and support? Is life asking you to give up some of your directed movements and trust the unknown? Allow these new thoughts and qualities to be translated through your movements. Let your dance evolve to include these changes. Continue moving for another five to ten minutes. Notice the changes to your dance, but also make sure that you retain the essential core of who you are. Also do not be afraid to add movements that at first may be uncomfortable or unfamiliar to you. Expansion always involves some risk. See if you can entertain that risk by giving yourself permission to literally move into the unfamiliar. See what changes and what remains the same. Trust your body to move you.

Closure

Let your movements come to an end. You may remain standing or in your last position, and for a few moments just feel the pulse of movement inside of you as your external movements come to a closure. Gently close your eyes again and become aware of the natural rhythm of your breath. Retain your experience. Let each cell of your body reverberate with the present energy that you sense in your body. You may lie back down on the floor, sit or remain standing. Take a few minutes for this.

You will now repeat the inventory that you did at the beginning of the session. Be aware of your physical body. Notice if you feel differently than when you started. How? What are the sensations in your body? How does your energy feel? (Pause) Now check in with your mental state. Is your mind quiet? What are the qualities of your thoughts? How is your mental state different then earlier? (Pause) Move on to your emotional state. Observe the colors in your emotional palette. Are there more feelings available to you now? What are they? How have they changed? How do you feel different? (Pause) Then once again identify with the witness. Locate it physically and feel the part of you that is connected to spirit, to your source of knowledge and vision, and that is steady and grounded. Take a couple of minutes to do this inventory mentally without judgment, and then return to observing your breath for a few more minutes.

Journaling

Feeling fully grounded in your body, with your boundaries intact, gently sit up and get your journal and pen. Begin to write. Let your hand flow without censoring anything. Write about your experience in the session and how you feel after it. Express how it felt to warm up the body part by part. What stood out for you in the creative exploration section? Did you find yourself discovering new ways to move? What was it like to express yourself through movement? What changed for you as you projected yourself into the future? Were you surprised by some sensations? Did you feel like time just flew by? Were you able to trust your body and the energetic impulses? What was easy? What was difficult? Were there any changes in your physical, mental, and emotional states after you completed the session? Can you still feel the connection to the witness?

Don't worry about grammar or repetition. Do not strain. You may write for as long as you'd like. Most importantly, stay connected to the feelings and sensations in your physical body and trust your observations and insights.

Points to Remember

This session can be repeated daily or as often as you like. Each time you do this session be prepared to discover something new. It is both the warm up and the foundation for all the other exercises in the book. Through Movement for the Mind you will not only become more comfortable with your body as a creative vehicle, but you will learn how to listen to and increase your body awareness. The more attuned you become to the language of your body, the more easily you will be able to decipher and utilize the knowledge that lies within.

In the following four chapters, you will be able to apply the principles in this session to unfold other themes. Before each exercise, I suggest that you warm up the body with the first three sections of this session. As you become more familiar and comfortable with using the movement vocabulary, and if time is an issue, you can skip those sections and go directly to the exercises at the ends of Chapters Three through Six.

Movement for the Mind is your passport to unfolding a world of creativity, psychological awareness, healing, and stress relief that begins in the body and translates to your life.

Chapter 3:
Creating Calm in the Midst of Chaos
– Dance as Stress Management

"Dancing is not getting up painlessly like a
speck of dust blown around in the wind.

Dancing is when you rise above both worlds,
tearing your heart to pieces, and giving up your soul.

Dance where you can break your self to pieces
and totally abandon your worldly passions.

Real men dance and whirl on the battlefield;
they dance in their own blood.

When they give themselves up, they clap their hands;

When they leave behind the imperfections of the self, they dance.

Their minstrels play music from within;
and whole oceans of passion foam on the crest of the waves."

— Rumi

Jane came to see me because of a significant weight problem. Her whole life was focused on food, her obesity, her discomfort with her body, and the stress that this problem was causing her both physically and emotionally. The pressures at work and home only exacerbated her problems.

At work she was under constant pressure to perform under deadlines and when she came home from work, her family demanded her attention. She became short tempered, easily upset, and found herself wanting to eat more. "I need some peace, some time to myself," she confided to me. "The only escape I get is eating, but in the long run that only makes things worse." Jane felt like she was both trapped by the demands of her world and by the way she reacted to them.

Certain types of stress are a positive and necessary part of living. For example, without the exertion of stress on our bones they would not grow.

In this chapter, however, we will focus on the kind of mental and emotional stressors that accompany our technological, fast paced, and highly competitive lifestyles plus the pressures that we each take on personally that can lead to a mental overload and eventually break down our health. As Jane realized, the stressful structure of her life was compounding her underlying problems with her body and not allowing her time to come up with alternative creative solutions.

Although for some it is preferable and necessary to also change their lifestyles and external conditions, we will primarily look at ways of altering our internal state to alleviate stress rather than how to change and manipulate the external environment. The exercise at the end of this chapter incorporates the principles discussed in the following pages.

Understanding Stress from the Inside-Out

Stress has become one of the main causes of disease and death in modern Western society. Medical researchers have found that it can contribute to cardiovascular disease, cancer, immune deficiency diseases, and can make us more prone to everything from the common cold to becoming accident prone and vulnerable to psychological disorders including depression. Yet, we think that just hearing a lecture on managing stress is going to resolve the situation for us. We have become so accustomed to learning and processing information intellectually, and ingesting pills as a medical remedy that we have forgotten the missing ingredient to making it all work, our participation.

I remember the first of several seminars that I gave called *Creating Calm In The Midst Of Chaos*. I was one of about fifty presenters in a large three day New Age conference. The room filled with people and I introduced some of the principles that we were going to explore in the seminar. Everyone sat attentively until I mentioned that I was going to be facilitating them into changing the role of stress in their lives. I added that I would not only be lecturing, but that I expected them to participate in the process. At that point about a third of the people left the room. After I regained my composure, I actually began to laugh as I realized the absurdity of what had just happened.

No matter how many books we read, lectures we listen to, or how much information we process, we still need to apply and live the principles learned. Taking a passive approach towards resolving stress will not relieve it. Memorizing stress management techniques will not necessarily translate them into practice. We can learn what not to do and what practices actually relieve stress, but without physically applying them they remain inert ideas.

Some of the most significant research being done about the effects of stress and how to counterbalance the negative impact is in the field of Psychoneuroimmunology (PNI) which I mentioned briefly in Chapter One. Candace Pert, scientist and author of *Molecules Of Emotion: Why You Feel The Way You Feel*, has been instrumental in isolating chemicals in the brain (neuropeptides) that talk to the whole body. Pert has been able to show the link between our mental, emotional, and physical states, and how these chemical responses happen inside of us.

Michael Murphy, human potential leader and author of *Kingdom Of Shivas Irons* coined the phrase that "we are each the bartender of our own souls." What that means is that we have the potential to create stress hormones called glucocorticoids and the ability to counteract them with mood altering hormones called opiopeptides. In other words, the possibility for relieving stress lies within each of us.

Although external situations and problems are often the source of stress, most of our capacity to control stress depends upon how we respond mentally, emotionally, and physically to these circumstances and events. Even when we can change stressful external situations, including our own physical habits, relieving stress is primarily an internal process. Being aware that we have a choice as to how we can respond to stressful situations gives us more control over stress than we could ever imagine; especially since most of us have been taught to manipulate outer conditions in order to control and change things in our lives. In this chapter, we will explore how Mindful movement can change the negative effects of stress from inside out. Learning to work with Movement for the Mind principles will allow you to look at a lot of the stress in your life from a perspective that puts you back in the driver seat.

Jane's Story

Jane understood the severity of her problem, and that her future health was in jeopardy. She had lost and regained over two hundred pounds in previous years. She had sought medical advice, had a personal trainer, and was in private and group therapy. She was considering repeating a liquid diet program to lose the weight, but realized that if she did not get to the root of her problems, she would simply regain the weight back as she had done before. She knew she felt stressed and disconnected from her body, but didn't know how to re-establish that integrity.

As uncomfortable as Jane was with her body, she loved movement and knew she needed to engage her body as well as her intellect in order to move beyond her blocks and the stress that it was causing her. Jane and her therapist had begun to look at her childhood and her relationship with her mother as one of the causes for her weight problems. Her therapist suggested that she was using food to compensate for the nurturing she never received from her mother. Yet, there was something in Jane's voice and in her body language that made me question if this really was the underlying cause for her problems.

In the movement sessions she discovered that before the age of twelve, she was a happy-go-lucky child. She was not bone thin, but average for her age without any concerns about her body or food. At the age of twelve her brother, who up to that time had been the center of her mother's attention and worries, left home. It was then that her mother shifted her attention to Jane and Jane's body. Her mother was obsessed with her own looks and weight and unfortunately projected those feelings onto Jane. Jane was placed on a diet and told that she had to lose weight or that she would develop a problem.

In the Movement for the Mind sessions, Jane got in touch with the twelve year old who hated feeling restricted by the diets and regime she was forced to follow. "I became the problem child in my family after my brother left. I felt confused and began to believe that something was very wrong with me." She remembered that food had to be sneaked, because her mother kept much of the food in a locked cupboard. Instead of using food as a nurturing substitute, she ate because everyone "told" her that she had a problem. She began to feel destined and resolved to being fat. It was only after this period that Jane actually developed a weight problem.

What came out of these sessions was also the realization that at the core of her problem was an internal schism. By succumbing to her mother's beliefs and to the pressures in her environment, Jane had lost her own voice and most significantly her sense of integrity. She was terribly uncomfortable in her body, but had no point of reference on how to feel differently. She had lost her inner connectedness and consequently any attempt to lose weight was sabotaged by the beliefs that were instilled in her as a child. She automatically rebelled against restriction, and internally believed that she was destined to have a weight problem.

In the Movement for the Mind sessions, Jane learned how to listen to herself and to re-instill an inner congruity. The process unfolded in several stages. Learning how to trust herself and to realize that nothing was wrong or had been wrong with her, allowed Jane to restore an inner level of integrity. Integration for Jane meant regaining control over her own body and shedding not only the pounds, but the beliefs about herself that were keeping stress at very high levels in her life. It also meant creating time for herself and being able to change the way she handled the pressures at home and at work. Retaining her integrity set the stage for creating a supportive environment in order to both lose weight and support a renewed image and experience of herself.

Signs of Stress

Living in an age where technology and the intellect are given prominence, we often pay a price at the physical, emotional, or spiritual level. Although stress is often associated with physical illness, mental, emotional, or spiritual triggers can precede it.

The signs of stress can happen on any of these levels. Let's look at some examples. Mentally, you may be on overload. Thoughts racing, taking on too many projects, or trying to figure everything out in advance can make you feel like you are spinning your wheels. Emotionally you may feel raw. It does not take much to push you over the edge. You find yourself crying or getting angry easily. Physically, you may be exhausted. You may feel like you have no energy, or that you are in high gear and on an adrenaline rush. Either way you are off-balance. Spiritually you may feel bankrupt. Your heart may feel heavy or dry like the desert.

The early signs of stress are sometimes subtle, and if we are moving too fast or unconsciously in our lives we may miss these early warnings. The key is to become more aware of the subtleties that cause us to feel scattered, off-balanced, overwhelmed, high strung, injury prone, nervous, depressed, and out of sorts.

Take a few moments now to write down some of your own stress signals. Especially note the signs that you may have taken for granted or that you have become accustomed to. The more aware that you become to what is happening inside of you, the greater control you can have over the quality of your life externally. We will now go over the keys to managing stress and how you can personally apply them in your life.

Four Keys to Managing Stress Through Movement for the Mind

Movement for the Mind activates four keys to managing stress: Integration, Breath, Expression, and Separation. While a variety of methods that offer techniques for stress management also use some of these keys, Movement for the Mind incorporates them simultaneously. The first key is the cornerstone and holds the foundation for the benefits that we can realize.

1. Integration

Stress can cause us to feel like a fragmented object, pulled in a dozen directions. We can lose our center, our sense of balance, and even our integrity. The word integrity comes from the same root as integrate, meaning to make whole or renew. Integrity requires that we bring all the pieces of our lives and ourselves — physical, mental, emotional, and spiritual — together to form a whole. It asks us to be responsible and accountable for the quality of our lives and to be true not only to others, but to ourselves. We cannot have integrity with others unless we first uphold integrity within ourselves.

To regain our sense of center and integrity requires a discipline that addresses who we are in its entirety. Movement for the Mind pulls us back to our center. We begin with body awareness and then engage the mind, emotions, and spirit in each session. This allows for a sense of unity and integrity and builds a basis for observing the dynamics and causes of stress and for alleviating them.

Although stress and the situations that cause stress are unique to each individual, one of the first places that stress shows up is usually the body. Whether the cause is mental, emotional, or physical, the body reflects and sometimes holds on to an event long after it is over.

For example, at the age of fifty-three, Marilyn Van Derbur Atler (a former Miss America) still suffered from the long-range effects of child abuse and the ensuing emotional and mental stress on her body. She could not fall asleep without medication. Her musculature system had become so used to staying tight and rigid in fearful anticipation of her abuser, that she still suffered severe muscle spasms and tension in her body roughly forty years after the abuse had stopped. Only after years of recovery was she able to tolerate the tension without feeling excruciating pain. Her body had incorporated tension and physical stress as the norm.

I recently responded to dental surgery with a similar but less extreme physical reaction. It was a simple one-hour skin graft procedure, but the anticipation of what the dentist was going to do and what I might feel sent my body into physical tremors. As I sat in the chair my heart raced. I began to take deep breaths and I was able to slow my heart rate, but I could not control my quivering jaw. My entire body shook for the hour the dentist worked on me and the quivering lasted another half hour after the procedure was over. Even though I knew how to reduce the imminent stress by meditating and by taking slow deep breaths, my body responded to my fear automatically. I watched with fascination as my body spontaneously reacted to my mental apprehension. Had I been able to get out of the dentist's chair and work with my body to feel the fear and subsequent tremors, to allow them expression, and then to bring in a new image that could support the successful completion of my surgery, I would probably have had a different experience in the chair.

Because the body is where stress shows up, it must be included in the process of stress reduction. This is why endurance training and other forms of exercise as well as yoga are now recommended in the combat of stress. However, as the findings of PNI show, our attitude and mental state also affects our level and experience of stress. Movement for the Mind starts with the body, but also incorporates mental and emotional images to stimulate a conscious integrated connection.

Even though as humans we are one unified system, in our Western culture, we act and are often treated as if we are fragmented. To utilize merely mental techniques or physical methods for treating stress-related disorders is as absurd as bringing just your brain to your therapist or your torso and legs to your personal trainer. Integration is the key. As we apply techniques that encourage integration, some of the major symptoms of stress are eliminated including feeling spread too thin, disjointed, and disconnected from ourselves.

While moving, a mysterious and yet predictable experience occurs not unlike in meditation. The mind calms down and we are able to focus our attention into the moment. Because Movement for the Mind also invokes a theme or point of reference, we create conscious movement. Integration thus happens on two levels. The first unfolds passively through the technique itself — the use of movement, music, mental images, and the experience of various emotions. The second aspect of integration occurs actively through journaling or sharing in a debriefing session. Individuals experience a sense of connectedness and the relationship to oneself is strengthened.

As in Jane's case, part of the remedy for stress is in repairing the rift that we feel inside of ourselves. Even though outer conditions may be the imminent cause of our experience of feeling wired, overloaded, and out of sorts, creating a level of integrity even for a moment can resuscitate us. Consciously practicing integration by working with the body, mind, emotions, and spirit stimulates an inner response. To manage stress effectively that inner response is essential. And as with anything, practice allows us to improve a skill and to make it familiar. To create integration we must practice in order to experience it as a continuum in our lives.

In Movement for the Mind integration occurs spontaneously and without strain as we engage our senses and direct our creativity toward a purpose. Inherent in the practice is the blending of parts of ourselves. We are not just bodies moving, or minds cluttered with deadlines and responsibilities. We are consciously participating, feeling, and moving energy.

2. Breath

In Yoga, the ancient philosophical system that originated in India, a great deal of attention is given to the breath. Referred to as Prana, meaning life force, the breath is consciously used to both quiet the mind and purify the body. Great Yogis, practitioners of Yoga, are able to master the mind and physical body through control of the breath. The breath is seen as the link between matter and spirit. By practicing various breathing techniques that concentrate both on the retention and expansion of the breath, Yogis enter an altered state of consciousness that bring states of bliss and the capacity to regulate their heart rates and other bodily functions.

In the West, we are just beginning to understand the significance of the breath in maintaining optimal health and in managing stress. Although learning how to breathe properly may seem like an oxymoron, it is an imperative tool in managing stress. Not only does deep breathing increase oxygen to the cells, but it can also slow one's heart rate and calm the mind. There are also subtle benefits that pertain to energy patterns in the body causing a sense of peace and well-being not unlike the experience of Yogis.

In Movement for the Mind, attention to the breath is vital. Many of my therapy clients have shared that the restrictions they feel in their bodies are often centered in the chest area. They report a difficulty in being able to take full or complete breaths and feel as if something emotionally is being held back in their breath. Many people experience a similar sensation by automatically holding their breath or barely breathing when they feel anxious or frightened.

In every session, the breath is called upon as the rhythm keeper. Rhythm, one of the *Dance Principles*, is generated inwardly through the conscious awareness of the flow of the in breath and the out breath. This stimulates a freedom of movement that also loosens old stuck somatic patterns.

Bodyworkers and practitioners of breathwork use specific breathing exercises in their work to accomplish similar results and to free body memories and physical limitations. For example, in Holotropic Breath Work, participants are taught a method of inhaling and exhaling through the mouth that can trigger past memories and stimulate strong feelings and emotions so that they can be released. In Movement for the Mind, the breath is used as a natural and interactive process that weaves body, mind, emotions, and spirit creatively together.

The breathing that is awakened through Movement for the Mind seems to activate a re-connection not unlike spiritual rebirth. It is like coming home, this time safely in the body. The *complete breath* technique that you learned in Chapter Two has two purposes. The first is to ground you in the body. In the same way that Yogis use the breath to master the body to achieve altered states and "out-of-body" experiences, the complete breath allows you a deepening, expanding experience while in the body. The *complete breath* begins to challenge us to use the diaphragm more fully and to identify this broadening experience in the whole body.

The second purpose of the *complete breath* is to become awake to and to utilize the natural rhythm of the breath as a point of awareness for creating one's own movement patterns. Many meditation techniques use the breath as a focal point for calming and focusing the mind. Every time the mind wanders, one gently brings one's thoughts back to the flow of the in breath and the out breath. The breath acts as a point of reference and concentration. Similarly, in Movement for the Mind, breathing awakens consciousness of the body's innate rhythmic and energy patterns. Most of us not only take our breathing for granted, but also are unaware of our internal rhythms, biological, energetic or emotional. Sadly, many people feel that they don't have any rhythm. A student in one of my fitness classes would announce before every class, "I was born without rhythm and I still don't have any."

If you feel that you don't have rhythm or if you would like to experience your body's innate rhythm and energy, take a moment to do this exercise. This is similar to a dance therapy technique called *Authentic Movement* that uses spontaneous movement without music to awaken the subconscious and stimulate the emotional body. (Read the instructions a couple of times and then just repeat them to yourself mentally.)

Stand up. Close your eyes and take four complete breaths and then continue breathing normally. Remember to keep breathing through your nostrils. Now begin to listen to the rhythm of your breath and see how your body responds energetically. You may begin swaying or rocking. Let movements occur spontaneously. Go with any impulse. If your body does not move, continue listening to the breath for a few more moments. Do not strain or try to make anything happen. The point is to let go and become more sensitive to the subtle rhythms inwardly.

If you felt your body moving at all, you may have also become aware of your heartbeat and the rhythm of that pulsation. Listening to these simple rhythms helps us to connect to ourselves and to the moment. It also allows us to move and respond more spontaneously and with less restriction and judgment. The rhythm of the breath in this way is used to quiet and focus the mind and to awaken us to the subtle energies within us. In Movement for the Mind, we can use this awakening for various purposes. The process alone of pausing to breathe deeply and then observing the breath will relieve the imminent effects of stress, but we can take this alleviation further.

3. Expression

The only bad or harmful feeling or emotion is one that is repressed and stagnant. (Although some people distinguish between emotions and feelings, I refer to them interchangeably.) Most of us would rather avoid a painful feeling rather than deal with it or express it. Many of us learned how to hide or repress our feelings out of survival as children. In Western cultures, boys are still taught not to cry or show any emotion. As adults we repeat these emotional patterns and when stress builds, we often are unequipped to deal with the accompanying feelings.

In a medical study cited by David Sobel, M.D., Regional Director of Patient Education and Health Promotion at Kaiser Permanente, which was conducted on survivors of cardiovascular diseases and heart attacks, researchers found that the number one way to prevent recurring cardiovascular problems was not through diet or exercise, but by releasing feelings of anger and resentment. Those patients who were able to change their attitudes and transform or let go of negative feelings were more likely to remain healthy than any other group.[2]

Part of the reason that great athletes are able to perform under tremendous competitive pressure and stress is because of their mental and emotional commitment, and the expressive release that their sport provides. Artists can thrive under deadlines and long hours of practice and work, and emerge renewed and

---

[2] Sobel, David. Lecture on Healthy Pleasures. San Francisco, September 30, 1995.

transformed due to the creative act. Creativity makes us feel alive, purposeful, and it nurtures our soul.

Creative expression — the backbone of Movement for the Mind — is equally important as a tool for managing stress. In a Movement for the Mind session, creative expression has three functions. The first is to explore one's creativity through the body. The second is to release stagnant thoughts, feelings, and energy and to express specific emotional states and issues. The third function is to literally use expression as movement: To allow moods and feelings the freedom to change shape and space. We will examine each function separately, although they often occur simultaneously in any session.

Exploring Creativity in the Body

One of the symptoms of stress is feeling out of balance. It may be as a result of working long hours, over-extending oneself, or having too many responsibilities and feeling spread too thin. Taking a half an hour, or even a few minutes in a day to explore creative movement can interrupt that pattern and alter the experience of being off-balance and stressed.

Exploring movement creatively serves two purposes. Because it is physical exercise, it provides all of the benefits of a workout. The heart rate increases, causing more blood flow and oxygen to the cells, and endorphins are released. Thoughts are absorbed in the flows of movement, thereby freeing the mind of external concerns. When you are creating movements you cannot also be worrying about your problems. The moment demands all of you. To be creative means that you are birthing something new; in this instance it is yourself. Out of the moment may come a new idea, a solution to your problems, or simply a much-needed reprieve that can return you to the demands in your life refreshed and more peaceful.

Individuals have often come up to me after a lecture or

seminar and confided that the way they relieve stress is to go into a room, close the door, put on music, and dance their hearts out. One woman assured me "it's better than Prozac. Your body releases the pent up energy, your mind and emotions are free in the moment of anxieties or pressing problems. The dance takes you over." For individuals who feel that they don't know how to dance, The *Movement for the Mind* CD or download is an easy introduction.

Expressing Emotions

The fastest way to transform negative emotions is to express them creatively: to give them an arena to sound, shape, and move without hurting oneself or anyone else. Unexpressed emotions can fester like an old wound not properly cleaned. Stress can exacerbate these emotions causing us to feel out of control inwardly as well as in the circumstances in our lives. Sometimes it is appropriate to express our feelings directly thereby clearing the air, but often there is no one to vent these feelings to and frustration builds up adding internal tension to an already overloaded system.

Emotions are like weather; once they are expressed they change and move on. They are not unlike the tantrums of small children. Once the screams and kicks subside, the child peacefully goes back to his toys as if nothing had ever happened. If we take apart the word emotion we have "e -motion": energy in motion. To keep the energy moving in our emotions we need to have appropriate outlets of expression.

Many people workout to release pent up emotions, but feelings can also be expressed more directly and beneficially. In Movement for the Mind, specific feelings are identified and then given the opportunity to be fully expressed. Because movement is the tool for expression instead of words, the energy is not restricted or censored. There is no linear time to feelings, so that the emotions expressed may be about today or they may be left over from childhood. Using your body to express these feelings through your limbs provides not only a release, but also a first hand experience of the reality of emotions.

When you practice any of the exercises at the end of the chapters in Part Two, you will notice that you always feel differently and more aware of your emotional palette after the end of each session. Most of us are afraid of expressing "negative" emotions, because we think they may take over or last forever. When we actually give them a physical voice and a chance to be expressed without hurting ourselves or anyone else, these emotions shift; stored, pent-up energy is released.

We often hold on to resentment and anger because we have no safe channels to express the unpleasant sensations that also accompany being in a human body. Anger, sadness, grief, and fear are in themselves not necessarily negative. The negative impact is most often experienced when these emotions become stagnant and are held in. Expressing these feelings allows them to move to the next phase. The feelings may not disappear overnight, and they will certainly continue to pop-up in the course of our lives. The key is to keep them fluid. Like the weather, then, we can watch as the sky changes from stormy to sunshine.

Expression as Movement

Although most of us are aware intellectually that everything is made up of energy, few of us think or live according to this reality. Our tendency is to look at external situations and objects as solid, including our own bodies. When change occurs in my life, my initial reaction is to become rigid and resist instead of flowing with what is eventually always forward movement. Far too often, I forget this law of energy and movement.

Dance teaches us about the flow of energy in our bodies. In Movement for the Mind, we manipulate time, space, energy, motion, and rhythm (the *Dance Principles*) to better understand the stage of our lives. Stress is, in energetic terms, a back-log. We've overloaded our systems and feel off-balance, scattered, disconnected. Energetically we may feel like we're moving backwards, sideways, or even upside down. We may be moving so fast that, like a car out of control, we're desperately steering to keep from crashing. All of these experiences can be expressed physically.

In the process of moving mindfully, we can allow these moods, feelings, and energy flows the freedom to express, explore and change shape, space, and dimension. We not only release stagnant thoughts and feelings, we allow them to evolve in an organic and self-contained manner.

In Movement for the Mind, one experiences the same flow as in nature. For example, water can be danced free and flowing, turned to ice and then re-experienced in its fluid state. One can experience the strength of a mountain or the porous, soft sediment of sand. One can dance feeling the weight of a thousand pounds and move with the lightness of a feather. In Movement for the Mind, emotional states are transformed by the manipulation of energy flows in the body.

Concurrently, one can dance the experience that the stressful events are creating and then purposefully change the environment energetically. For example, imagine that you just broke up with your mate. You're working ten hours a day and still don't know how to make ends meet. You've just gone to the dentist for a routine visit and find you need major dental work. The list goes on. You're feeling lonely, exhausted, and on the verge of despair. The experience is physical and it is also mental, emotional, and spiritual.

You begin to move. Weighted down by the circumstances in your life, you move slowly, ponderously, feeling the massive weight on your shoulders. Your steps are hesitant. You crawl to the ground and move sideways on all fours. You keep adding movements that express how you feel and for these moments you let it all hang out. There is no one to impress or act like the hero for.

Then with your will, change your circumstance. Move as if the weight has been lifted and you feel lighter then you have in years. Move to high level and change tempos. Run, skip, jump, and then move slowly again. Feel that you have many choices. Notice that while crawling you can also move forward, backwards, and sideways. Replace the hesitant steps with ones that are direct and make you feel sure footed. Begin to delight in the variations and keep moving until you physically feel the energy shifting in your body.

Although nothing may have changed externally, in these few moments you have been able to impact your internal experience and seen the way energy moves and how you can direct the flow. Your body is just a microcosm of your larger world. The circumstances in your life can also change just as suddenly.

Having a direct experience of our energetic reality can help us to cope when things seem stuck and overwhelming. It is important to remember that when one moves, a process of creation takes place that is embodied and that can be referred back to over and over again in the body. We can physically re-pattern the experience and thereby affect the outcome. We are changing our attitudes, visualizing the results, and experiencing the shift in our bodies. In this instant movement becomes literal. Stress is so often all consuming. It feels like life will never be different. Movement for the Mind allows us to experience the possibility of feeling different, and to see that change and movement do happen. The old proverb that "this too shall pass" is directly experienced in the body.

4. Separation

The fourth key to managing stress is to experience that the stressful circumstances are distinct from who we are. More often than not, we identify with the stress in our lives and unconsciously take on the effects as if they were a part of our bodies. In the exercise at the end of this chapter you will have an opportunity to experience a stressful situation in your life as separate from yourself. As simplistic as this may sound, most of the damage caused by stress is due to the way we identify and internalize our circumstances.

In Vipassana, a form of Buddhism, students are taught that they are not their thoughts, and learn to become detached from them by watching dispassionately as thoughts arise and subside while they sit for meditation. Several other forms of Eastern philosophy build their teachings around the principle of detachment. By not identifying who we are with what happens to us, whether it is great or tragic, we can remain steady and peaceful. By learning to be watchful rather than reactive, we can allow life to flow without having to make judgments or grab at every twist and turn.

However, when stress hits whether it is due to the loss of a job or home, long commute hours, mounting bills, not enough sleep or a combination of circumstances, it's hard to stay detached. Yet, we need to realize that we are not our stress or our chaos and that we have a choice as to how we internally hold the events that happen to us. This choice is like the difference between gashing your arm and just tearing your clothes. One hurts your body while the other only damages what you are wearing. Stress merely damages our clothes unless we internalize the injury.

Carolyn Myss, New Age author and teacher, claims that the circumstances in our lives that we identify with cost us our energy. For every event that we feel tied to whether it is an emotional wound from the past or an uncomfortable situation in the present, we lose a portion of our life force energetically to these circumstances. Eventually they can cost us our health. We can agree intellectually and tell ourselves that we shouldn't let these things bother us, but for most of us the response is automatic. We need to learn to experience this truth in our bodies.

This does not mean that you become indifferent to others or cut off your feelings and emotions. Instead it requires you to be aware of and present to your boundaries and the choices that you make. The best preventative medicine is to catch yourself before the stress becomes overwhelming and causes physical or emotional damage.

In the exercise that follows you will notice what is going on internally. Most of us know what stress costs us, but sometimes we can be so caught up in the momentum of our lives that we ignore the signs of stress. In this exercise, we energetically change the effect that the circumstances are causing us. While moving, we mentally place the circumstances, events, and situations in front of us, separating them physically and mentally from our bodies. The power of the mind brought together with the body can cause shifts that can make a difference between illness and health.

For example, not only was regaining integrity an important breakthrough for Jane, but working with the principle of separation allowed her to shift her pattern of obesity. Trying to escape the pressures at work and at home, worrying about her weight, thinking about food, and eating consumed her from morning to night. She identified who she was with her problems. It was not until she separated who she was from her stress that she was able to lose the weight she desired and to keep it off. For Jane it was not just a matter of changing her eating habits, but changing her physical, emotional, and mental habits. Realizing that she no longer had to carry the mental and emotional baggage from her childhood allowed her to release her obsession, ask for the support that she needed, and become the woman she'd always wanted to be.

Exercise: Creating Calm in the Midst of Chaos

Managing stress may be one of the single most important commitments that you make in your life. Whether stress is an infrequent or isolated occurrence for you or part of your everyday existence, the principles described in this chapter can alert you to the early signs of feeling off-balanced, obsessed, or overwhelmed, and can help you restore an inner experience of peace.

Before you begin the following exercise, take a moment to review the four keys and ask yourself these questions:

- **Integration:** What does integration mean to you? In what part of your life could use more integrity? Where are you feeling off-balanced? How could you restore this balance?

- **Breath:** Do you find yourself holding your breath frequently or breathing shallowly? Are you frightened easily or do you carry a lot of tension in your chest? See if you can practice the *complete breath* five minutes in the morning and five minutes before you go to sleep at night.

- **Expression:** What is the level of expression in your life? Do you easily express your feelings? Do you sometimes feel like you might explode with rage or frustration? Do you have creative outlets so that you can safely express yourself?

- **Separation:** Do you closely identify with the events that happen to you? Do you notice if things eat you up on the inside or are you easily able to let go of people, situations, or events that cause you hurt or annoyance?

After answering these questions, look at which areas of your life could use expansion or correction. Remember awareness is the first step towards change and can help you prevent future problems from occurring.

The following exercise is to be used to identify the issues that are causing you stress, and to help you release and manage their negative effects. Please use the Self-Awareness section, including the breathing, boundary, and inventory, as a tool to actively think about and use the keys of Integration, Breath, Expression, and Separation. Remember that reading the chapter will give you understanding, but doing the exercises will give you the results and experience of these principles.

If you have the time, you'll want to first warm up with the movement vocabulary. Once you are familiar with the *Dance Principles,* Warm Up, and Creative Exploration then you can go on to this section. Before you begin the session survey your room and make sure you have the privacy and space that you need without bumping into anything. Any room will do as long as you can stretch out and take several large steps in all directions. Take off your shoes, place them out of your way, and then leave your voice of judgment (VOJ) with your shoes.

After you have completed the exercises, write down the feelings, memories or any other impulses that you may have experienced while moving. The most important point is to let your body do the communicating and to not judge or censor any of the movements or feelings. Stay aware of your reactions and your boundaries.

Again remember to read the entire section through once and then you may want to record the instructions and move to the sound of your own voice pausing in the appropriate places to give yourself time to complete each task.

Musical Selections: Feel free to add music to your sessions. Remember that music is a motivator, it can support the environment that you are creating or it can work against it like a distraction. There will be two sections in this session. Make sure that the selections are easily accessible so that there is minimal distraction when you change the music for Section II. Stay connected to your feelings as you change the music. For the first section I would like you to choose a piece of music that is dissonant, discordant, and even chaotic. You can use *Bell Born* by Michael Mantra. For the second section choose music that is calming and pleasant and makes you feel peaceful, yet energetic, and joyful. Yanni's, *In my time, Shamanic Dream,* or *Elysian Beaches,* produced by Tranquil Technology Music, are good selections. Or use any favorite piece of music.

Breathing

Find a spot in the room that you feel comfortable in and have the physical dimensions to move in all directions without bumping into anything. Lie down on your back with your feet straight in front of you and your arms comfortably by your side. Close your eyes.

Begin now by taking some deep complete breaths the way you were instructed in Chapter Two for at least five rounds and then allow the natural rhythm of your breath to return. Just observe the natural rhythm of your breath for another five rounds. Allow this natural flow of the in breath and the out breath to be the gage for the rhythm in your movement patterns.

Boundaries

Become aware of your physical boundaries. You will define your physical boundaries through the skin on the surface of your body, which differentiates you from the floor, the air, the music, and even the instructions in this section. Touch your skin with your hands so that you know where your body's surface begins and ends. Make sure there's no place on your skin that is numb or undefined where you can disassociate from your body. Take as long as you need to identify your outer boundaries thoroughly. (Pause)

Once you have defined your physical boundaries, mentally go inside your skin and make the space on the inside as spacious and secure as you can conceive. There should be no feelings of restriction here. These are your inner boundaries. It is here that you can safely house your memories, feelings, dreams, images, and inner child. No one can judge, change or invalidate this place within your outer boundaries.

Physical, Mental, Emotional, and Spiritual Inventory

Now be aware of your physical body. Notice any heat or cold, comfort or discomfort. Be aware of your energy level. Do you feel tired or invigorated? Do not feel like you have to change anything. Just observe your physical body without judgment for thirty seconds to a minute. Change your focus to your mental state. Is your mind quiet or full of chatter? What is the quality of your thoughts? Simply observe your mental state for about thirty seconds. Now check in with your emotional state. What feelings are available to you right now? Sadness? Joy? Anger? Numbness? Neutrality? Without judging just notice what you feel. Last but not least become aware of the witness. It is the part of you that no matter what you have gone through is always OK. It is the knower in you who remembers your dreams. You may also call this part source, spirit, or soul. Locate the witness somewhere in your physical body. You may find it in your heart, solar plexus, or anywhere else.

Section 1: Identifying your Chaos

After you have warmed up with the Movement Vocabulary in Chapter Two and feel ready to proceed, close your eyes again. You may be sitting, standing, or lying down. Begin to picture what is causing you stress. It may be a work situation, a relationship issue, or it may be a combination of little things that have finally added up to being too much for you to handle. If you are experiencing the loss of a loved one, it may simply be a matter of time for you to have these feelings. Use your discretion to know when it is time to feel the grief, pain, and loss, and when it is time to let go.

Now bring not only the situation that is causing you stress to mind, but also begin to feel and play up your reactions to the situation. Express the stress through your emotions, and then begin translating these feelings into movement. Let yourself respond, react, emote, and evoke the stress that you feel so that your entire body and its movements become the embodiment of stress. Let yourself go, but as always stay within the range of physical safety. You may keep your eyes closed unless you are traveling around the room, then make sure you open them so that you don't bump into anything. Continue moving, allowing your movements to crescendo and peak at least once (about ten to fifteen minutes).

Section II: Creating Calm

At your peak, first mentally and then physically release the stress from your body. Place it in front of you, making sure the impulses are now energetically outside your body. As you listen to these instructions while moving, you will feel the stress literally leaving your body and you may even "see it" in front of you. (Pause) Let the stress and emotions remain outside of you. Notice that they are still present, but they are no longer housed inside of you.

Begin moving without the invasiveness of these stresses and their effects. Notice if and how your movements change. Replace these stressful emotions with your own energy and movements. Let your dance blossom rekindling your own essence and sense of self. Identify with your inherent traits and express them. Feel your joy, mischievousness, peacefulness, energetic qualities, and any other sensations that define you at your best and most comfortable. Dance for ten to fifteen minutes staying aware that the stressful situations in your life have not disappeared. Nothing outwardly may have changed except that now you are maintaining the integrity of your own energetic boundaries without letting the stressors be internalized.

Closure

Bring your movements to a closure by gently closing your
eyes and by becoming aware of the natural rhythm of your breath.
Retain your experience. Let each cell of your body reverberate with
the present energy that you sense in your body. As you do, check
in with the stressful circumstances but do not let them in. Merely
acknowledge their presence, and stay connected to the present
energy and feelings inside your body. Stay awake to the distinction.
You may lie back down on the floor, sit, or remain standing. Take a
few minutes for this.

We will now repeat the inventory that we did at the beginning
of the session. Be aware of your physical body. Notice if you feel
differently than when you started. How? What are the sensations
in your body? How does your energy feel? (Pause) Now check in
with your mental state. Is your mind quiet? What are the qualities
of your thoughts? How is your mental state different then earlier?
(Pause) Move on to your emotional state. Observe the colors in your
emotional palette. Are there more feelings available to you now?
What are they? How have they changed? Is the stress gone? (Pause)
Then once again identify with the witness. Locate it physically
and feel the part of you that is connected to spirit, to your source
of knowledge, and that is not internally affected by the stressful
circumstances in your life. Take a couple of minutes to do this
inventory mentally without judgment, and then return to observing
your breath for a few more minutes.

Journaling

Feeling fully grounded in your body, with your boundaries
intact, gently sit up and get your journal and pen. Begin to write
without censoring anything. Write about your experience in the
session. Talk about the stressful situations that you expressed and
what changed for you. What did you learn? How can you apply your

experience to the daily events in your life? What reminders can you use to help manage your stress levels?

Write about the four keys — Integration, Breath, Expression, and Separation — and how you experienced them. Were you able to feel a sense of integration and what it means to be in integrity with yourself? Does doing the *complete breath* and then focusing on the rhythm of your breath help to quiet your mind and emotions? How did it feel to express your stress and then release it from your body? Were you able to use the tool of separation? What other insights did you receive?

Like in the previous journaling section, just write. Don't worry about grammar or repetition. Do not strain. You may write for as long as you'd like. Most importantly, stay connected to the feelings and sensations in your physical body and trust your insights.

Points to Remember

This session can be repeated as often as you wish. Use it to manage your stress levels and as a reminder to not hold onto or internalize the negative effects of stress. In addition, practicing any of the movement sessions in this book will teach you about integration and keep your expression level high and your creativity open. It will help prevent the emotional stagnation and back log that can occur under stress.

Simply practicing the *complete breath* will relax you and allow you to quiet your mind when you feel like you are on mental overload. Moving to the rhythm of your breath will make you more aware of your inner rhythms and will help you become more sensitive to the language of your body.

Practicing these four keys is a reminder that energetically everything is contained within you. Even though stress may be a part of modern life, you can actively learn how to create calm in the midst of chaos.

Chapter Four:
Creativity Unbound —
Dance as Creativity

"Learning to walk sets you free —
learning to dance gives you the greatest freedom of all;
to express with your whole self the person that you are."
— *Melissa Hayden*

What is Creativity?

A dear friend of mine in her mid-fifties often laments, "Everyone around me is so creative but I have no creative skills." She does not consider her gardening skills, her sensitivity towards plants and flowers, and her decorative touches around her house as creative. Consequently, she consistently feels inferior to others. So many of us have been programmed to believe that we are not artistic or creative. Most of us have grown up in a culture that defines creativity by specific artistic skills rather than as a natural attribute given to everyone at birth that must be nurtured and developed like all other inherent qualities.

We're taught that if we don't have the "right" body or perfect skill, we cannot dance; if we didn't excel in art as a child, we cannot draw; if we're not poets or journalists, we cannot write; if we are not great orators, we cannot act. Our Western culture, by and large, reserves artistic expression for the few, not the masses. One of the greatest values of any art is its power to carry the individual beyond him or herself into an expanded world of imagination, creation, and understanding. Yet the notion that the very unfoldment of our lives holds artistic and creative potential is rarely fostered.

Encouraging and developing creativity is not an educational priority for the young or the old. We emphasize the importance of material success, intellectual prowess, and athletic skill without recognizing their creative roots. And yet creative moments are vital to these accomplishments as well as everything else we do in life. Creativity is a necessary part of leadership, problem solving, invention, productivity, excellence, and beauty. Without creative expression most of life would literally cease to exist. Creativity both demands and fosters inspiration. It allows us to feel alive and purposeful.

Creativity is often associated with expressing a particular talent, yet if we look at its root origin, it's meaning is much more encompassing. In English, the word "creativity" comes from the verb "create." To create conjures not only artistic images but also thoughts of birth itself. In fact "creating" connects us to God and to the life generating processes of the universe. It is in our acts of creation that we are closest to our creator. What leaders, inventors, visual artists, architects, craftspersons, writers, dancers, actors, musicians, engineers and designers, among many others, all have in common is the awareness of bringing forth something new. Even if it is a reconstruction or a replica, they engage in a process of birth, of creation.

When we open up to creative expression so much more in our lives becomes accessible to us. Not only do we discover latent talents, but also we free up fixed ways of thinking and behaving and awaken to the possibility of new thoughts and opportunities. It is in the act of becoming creatively aware that we embrace our capacity to be renewed.

Young children who are as yet untainted by compounded scars and rigid beliefs have this innate creative spark. They exhibit their creativity innocently and uninhibitedly. Their drawings, use of color, dances, and fantasies are not bound by static views of reality or by rules that define this image as correct and that color as wrong. Their imagination runs freely with their bodies. They are spontaneous and live in present time. Children laugh, cry, sing, jump, roll, crawl, run, skip, leap, and play. They are connected to the earth, the air, and to their inner imagination. Instead of directing this creative power, our educational and social systems tend to dilute it to the point of extinction. As soon as we are old enough to focus some of these creative expressions, their diversity and uniqueness fall prey to peer pressures and the demand to conform to what is judged as the norm. Intelligence becomes measured and creative freedom often gives way to "the basics," rote learning, and to voices of reason and conformity.

It is not surprising then, that our most creative geniuses including Einstein often failed their school subjects and never quite fit in with their peers. Many celebrated artists, great leaders, inventors, and other luminaries experienced themselves as outcasts and were even disclaimed as lunatics before they or their work was acknowledged. As adults most of us are cut off from our authenticity and creative curiosity. We also no longer use our bodies as expressive vehicles.

Creation Starts with the Body

As babies our first acts of creation come from movement itself. We reach out with fingers and toes, learning to touch and grasp. These first gestures of communication are our first introductions to dance. Although as babies and children we may not be making them up consciously, they are the means by which we first express ourselves. The language of the body holds our first attempts to communicate and define our boundaries. Later our movements become more complex as we add subtleties to our communications. We grow up and mature, but in the process many of us lose the creative connection to our bodies and to the rich inner landscapes that we resourced as young children.

In this chapter we will focus on three aspects of how Movement for the Mind can enhance our awareness, understanding, and application of creativity. The first aspect, using the body as a creative vehicle, is the foundation for using the other two. They are: expanding our perceptions and ability to see clearly, and combining Movement for the Mind with other nonverbal forms of expression. In addition, we will look at how Movement for the Mind can be used in diverse environments including academic and business settings to further extend our concepts and applications of creativity. The questions and exercises at the end of the chapter will help you define and enliven your own personal experience of creativity.

As a creative activity, Movement for the Mind restores our imagination, openness, exuberance, and sense of integration. Movement for the Mind demands involvement and focuses our attention to the present moment. Exploring our creativity non-verbally invites us to the edge and implores us to move from the ordinary to the extraordinary. It is part of our birthright to discover this edge within each of us.

Using the Body as a Creative Vehicle

Judy's Story

Judy, a computer programmer and analyst in her fifties, was acutely aware of a certain imbalance in her life. She had spent most of her life developing intellectual and analytical skills and felt disconnected from her creativity and what she called, her "feminine." Judy had practiced martial arts and began to pursue activities to awaken her feminine side. She participated in drumming circles, took painting classes, explored healing techniques such as Reiki and massage, but still felt dissatisfied. She shared, "There is something missing. It's as if I am pursuing all these creative activities, but I can't find my center. I am feeling more alive and vibrant, and yet I don't sense the integration that I yearn for." The one thing she had been afraid to pursue was dance. She felt like she had two left feet and that dance was out of her "artistic league."

After reading about Movement for the Mind in a newspaper article, she decided to take a creative risk and participate in a workshop.

In the workshop she discovered that she could "dance" and that by generating movements from within herself she could also experience the core of her movements. This caused her to connect to parts of herself that she had previously not recognized. Connecting creatively in her body had a dramatic effect on Judy's artistic expression. After the workshop, she went home and drew a pastel from images she had visualized during her dance. It was the first time that she had ever drawn anything without an external model. Her creative growth continued from that point on. Three years later I ran into Judy at a bookshop where she shared her creative breakthrough with me adding, "These days I feel like I am a fully creative, dynamic woman."

Sandy's Story

Sandy, the daughter of a friend of mine, was in her early twenties and pursuing a career as a professional singer. She was anxious about a particular audition, so her mother gave her the *Movement for the Mind* CD thinking that it might calm her nerves and increase her body awareness. Sandy liked how she felt when she did the exercises on the CD and began practicing these exercises daily for several weeks.

The audition went well and she was chosen as the lead singer. Sandy discovered that doing the sessions taught her how to be more comfortable in her body which affected the quality of her voice and her ability to project her presence more dramatically on stage. She had never trained as a dancer, but found that working with her body creatively increased her artistic range as a singer.

Jason's Story

Jason wanted to learn how to dance. He practiced judo at a studio about five hours a day and had also studied several other forms of martial arts. He was very physically fit, but felt socially awkward and thought learning to dance might make him more acceptable and less self-conscious around others.

At first he wanted me to teach him specific dance steps, but when we began working with Movement for the Mind and concentrating on the improvisational and creative components, Jason noticed unexpected results in various areas of his life. His judo improved. He became more agile and swift in his movements and gained a poise and balance that had not been there before. His experience with creative dance also extended into the daily activities of his life. He found himself opening up to people more easily and realized after several months of working together that he felt more comfortable with himself and consequently less awkward in his relationships.

Judy, Sandy, and Jason each used the Movement for the Mind sessions to expand their creative potential. Using the body creatively was not the end result, but a means for unfolding their specific talents and experiencing a more expanded sense of themselves. In the next story we see how the same principles can be applied creatively in a business environment.

Creative Problem Solving

Fortunately, creativity is being encouraged and programs are being implemented that allow for a more dynamic and innovative environment in various business settings. In some private corporations, I have been asked to work with the theme of creative problem solving. For example, one company wanted to create a mission statement that would reflect a fresh and authentic image. They wanted the words to have both life and meaning. Movement for the Mind was used as a tool for brainstorming.

Instead of brainstorming through words, participants engaged the body. After the warm up, we worked with the Dance Principles varying time, space, energy, motion, and rhythm much like physical doodling. At first it was just bodies engaging muscles, utilizing space, and moving at various levels and tempos. Like words flying through space in verbal discourse this was the opening process.

The next step was to direct the energy and brainstorming process. Using verbal cues that related to specific work issues, participants incorporated these themes into their movements. Instead of merely relying on the intellect for meaning and imagery, individuals were instructed to dance the message of the company, to create through movement the impulses and heartbeat of the company that they were a part of. There was no censoring or judgment. Each individual was allowed to express dynamically what words could only shadow. Concepts, ideas, and feelings converged through the body's language.

The last step was to translate the nonverbal experience into words and to write the mission statement. Sitting in a circle, participants discussed their physical exploration and experiences and as key words and sentences were jotted down, they created a dynamic mission statement. The mission statement took on an organic form and was not just an intellectual concept of what the company stood for. Their dances allowed them to experience the principles of the company first hand. The finished product became a living entity within each of them.

Although the goal was to brainstorm and to create a mission statement, the process rewarded each participant with much more. The consensus after the session was that each participant felt more relaxed and revitalized. They had tapped into a rich labyrinth of creative awareness that they utilized professionally and could benefit from personally.

The creative act of problem solving and brainstorming is most effective when we can combine the capacity for concentration and freedom of thought. Through an approach that is both spontaneous and guided, individuals experience what it is like to be fully present in the moment. Using the body as a creative vehicle allows us to align our minds and psyche and to be fully available for what comes. Creativity is most powerful in that moment-to-moment experience.

Expanding our Perceptions to See Clearly

Our perception of things not only influences our experience, but perceptions are often very subjective. What we see and how we see things can be influenced by habit as well as our mental, emotional, and physical state.

How often have you walked down a particular street and not noticed something until someone else pointed it out? Have you ever misjudged someone or a situation because it reminded you of something from the past? So many of us miss the obvious when we are mentally or emotionally pre-occupied. It can cloud our capacity to be open and receptive to the next creative step.

Expanding our perceptions is a lesson in seeing more attentively and clearly. It teaches us to be more present and to be more sensitive to the motivating factors behind what and how we see things. Observing how we view things is another tool to increase our creativity. When our vision is clear and open we are more receptive to ideas, feelings, and innovative possibilities.

A friend of mine knew a woman who had been blind since birth and suddenly began to see colors and shapes at the age of forty. Her renewed sight brought her an unexpected realization. Because she had been physically blind, she had developed the ability to see in other ways. She shared, "when I regained my vision I realized how little we truly observe if we only use our eyes and don't also engage our hands, ears, feet, heart, and soul. Our eyes only perceive what is in front of us, our body and soul sees what is beyond. To truly see we must go deeper than what is obvious."

In an academic course at Stanford University's Graduate School of Business called *Personal Creativity In Business*, students participate in Movement for the Mind sessions to engage the senses and to risk new ways of seeing while moving and observing the results. The primary purpose of the course is to awaken each student to his own inherent creativity. The students learn to "be creatively awake" as part of the path towards excellence and success in both the personal and professional areas of their lives. In these sessions they used movement as a metaphor for expanding their perceptions.

In the Movement for the Mind sessions, participants were free to explore their creative awareness through the body. They used the Dance Principles to awaken the language of the body. Leaving their voice of judgment with their shoes, participants expressed themselves without the fear of what they looked like or how they moved. As I mentioned in Chapter Two, the voice of judgment, is decidedly incompatible with creative expression. It is the voice of the inner critic responsible for censoring ideas and actions. The voice is like an internal angry parent or restrictive analyst that challenges our self-esteem and confidence. It is often the voice that squelches dreams with "Oh, you could never do that. You look ridiculous. You're not creative."

Once participants felt that they were "safe" and would not be judged for their movements, a sense of freedom and creative risk unfolded. In the warm up, much of their "seeing" was with their eyes closed which helped them to focus within and feel what was going on inside themselves. They moved in ways they had not dared to since their childhood. They discovered aspects of themselves and others in the room that had gone previously unnoticed. Many described an increased awareness of feelings and emotions that they normally chose to deny or ignore. By working with some of the opposite energy flows described in Chapter Two, using patterns that included large, small, strong, light, direct, indirect, slow, fast, bound and free movements, they had the opportunity to explore their "normal" physical modus operandi and to experience vastly different ways of moving.

In the session, participants were asked to identify movements that most expressed how they would describe themselves creatively. Instead of communicating who they were with words they danced their personalities and their essence. While maintaining their boundaries and without sacrificing their individual dance, they were then asked to mingle and connect with others non-verbally. Each of these varied movement sequences was accompanied with the verbal instructions to be aware of oneself, one's environment, and one's perceptions without judgment.

After connecting to others, students were asked to return to their own dance and to add a dimension to their movements that might bring them closer to their desired creative goals. For example, someone who found that they most identified with being strong, bound, direct, and fast might have added the dimensions of slow, light, and free to their movements. By including these dimensions they were not only adding new physical ways of moving, but also engaging the mental and emotional equivalents. For someone who was tightly wired, moving slower and freer naturally evoked a level of patience and flexibility. Even moving once in this manner gave individuals an experience that they may not have felt previously leading them to a creative choice for the future.

Participants had the opportunity to view themselves and others differently and more objectively. Part of expanding our perception is noticing how our view of the world and ourselves colors our ideas and creative potential. The more we can expand our vision, the greater our possibilities. Creativity is born out of innocence and freedom. It is not easily fostered under criticism or restriction. As we expand our own internal boundaries we allow new ways of seeing to occur within us. It begins a kinesthetic process that can then be transferred to very practical areas of one's life.

In the nonverbal spaces, the students saw themselves in a new light. One man shared, "I never thought of including my body in a creative process. I know that I'm intelligent and that I can excel mentally, but I never knew I could expand the space inside my mind through my body." Others commented, "Time seemed to stop, changing my perception. I felt like I was in a hypnotic state, relaxed, yet fully alert, and somehow altered." And some experienced an inner harmony that they did not know existed.

Expanding our perceptions allows us to interrupt our learning status quo and to tap into thoughts, feelings, and actions that might otherwise never have occurred to us. It teaches us to take risks, to be innovative, and to question rather then accept rote answers from others or ourselves. As we access our unique creative potential the possibilities for progress, invention, self-improvement, contribution, and material success are proportionately enhanced. The more awake we can be in the body, the more we can stretch beyond previously held boundaries and reach for these visions.

Team Building

In terms of creativity, we often find ourselves working alone. Most of us think of being creative as a solo experience. However, in many situations including community groups, school boards, classrooms or any other organization, teamwork is also necessary. Using Movement for the Mind for team building can offer a creative alternative to a complex issue that demands both individual brightness and group solidarity. When we are in a group, it is sometimes difficult to find a balance between our unique qualities and the group's needs. The challenge is to create an environment of interdependence where individuals can also reflect their strengths. Movement for the Mind gives us a direct physical experience of this creative process.

The warm up is especially significant for team building because individuals must define themselves before they can contribute as team members. The inventory allows us to check in, while the breathing and boundary work relaxes the body and calms the mind preparing us to be present and available to others.

In the exploration, participants have the opportunity to define and expand their own talents, skills, and strong points. This section focuses on the individual, allowing participants ample time to explore their own levels of unique contribution. Equally as important, they examine their weaker points without judgment. Although people may have similar roles, one person may be more creative while someone else may have stronger organizational skills. Both components are important to the functioning of the group as a whole. Everything is experienced kinesthetically. Participant's minds are alert with imagery while their senses are prompted by the music.

In the next stage, participants form dyads and triads similar to the section described in Chapter Two. Dyads are often easier to participate in than triads. The definition of one's boundaries extends to one's particular skill and role in the organization. By retaining these boundaries while interfacing with others, participants learn how to appropriately hold their own value while being receptive to others.

Beginning with the mirroring exercise, one person leads while the other follows; then they change until each individual has experienced both leading and following. They then progress to mutually communicating while staying in contact with each other visually and kinesthetically. Outwardly it looks like two bodies moving independently, yet the bond of contact is as important as the communication. The contact can be kept through the eyes, through touch, or energetically. The energetic connection is perhaps the subtlest and yet the one many of us respond to most easily and instinctually. Each of these forms of contact and communication help the participants to hone their interpersonal skills in a unique manner. By relying only on nonverbal forms of communication, they become aware of messages and signals that might otherwise be masked. They are forced to be more present with themselves and their partners.

Finally participants move into the stage where they are moving together as one team. They lead and follow, changing roles smoothly and spontaneously. They must stay conscious of their own boundaries and yet be willing to move in the moment sometimes leading, sometimes following, and at times being aware that there is only movement, as if there were no leader or follower. They then change partners and repeat the entire process beginning with the mirroring exercise.

After everyone has experienced at least two different partners, each group breaks up and they briefly move back into the individual dances that they developed at the start of the session. The last stage is to bring these roles back to the larger group and interact with others at will using any of the exercises to communicate. Some mirror each other, others move spontaneously together, and there are those who just move separately and yet connect in another way.

After about ten minutes of interacting, we bring closure to the movement session by returning to the awareness of breath, boundaries, and end with the inventory. The group then gathers in a circle for discussion and debriefing.

In terms of team building, it is of utmost importance to create an environment where individuals can feel purposeful as part of a larger whole. Each individual is given the opportunity to identify where he/she is best suited to contribute as an integral part of the team. In the Movement for the Mind session, the most significant interactions happen without words. Participants identify strengths and talents and then learn how to move and interact, harmonizing their skills with others.

In the debriefing process people shared their experiences. A participant in his fifties commented, "I have always preferred to work alone because I was afraid I'd have to give up my expertise and just follow someone else who may know less than me. Through the exercises I actually enjoyed teaming up with others, and I was surprised that moving together was so smooth and easy. It felt like we were just one person moving." Another person realized, "I always took it for granted that my job was basically to support others, but I never took pride in that role. Now I realize that what I do is significantly related to the end result of what we're working on. I feel good about my work and feel that I am really a part of this community." The debriefing session also brings up suggestions on how to further improve relations and team support. People then can divide into smaller groups to discuss specific ways of following through the ideas and experiences that have resulted from the session.

Movement for the Mind provides grounding for innovative and improved methods of working together. Movement taps into the unconscious and stimulates solutions to problems that may have remained hidden. Using Movement for the Mind for team building is a perfect match for combining a creatively dynamic approach that supports both individual diversity and a unifying goal. In a group setting, bringing nonverbal forms of creativity to a basically intellectual approach allows for more balance and innovation.

The Gift of the Nonverbal

When the head of the dance department at the University of Santa Clara asked me to give a workshop on creativity, I assumed that most of the participants were already rooted in the creative process because they were dancers. Yet, as I found out, many were as insecure and unsure of their creative potential as my friend who felt uncreative despite her decorative and gardening skills. Although dance challenges one's body, mind, psyche, and spirit, without confidence and an awareness of integration, one can still feel separate from the creative act. The experience of creativity comes from immersing ourselves in the act of creation. But we must also identify with and recognize this experience.

In a Movement for the Mind session, the debriefing portion is designed to help each person learn from, integrate, and then apply his or her own discovery and creative exploration. This part of the session is usually conducted through words — either spoken or written. Words provide an intellectual format that lends credibility and clarification to the process. Yet most people come to me as a result of their frustration with standard methods of learning and analysis. They find that just talking about their feelings and experiences does nothing to enhance or change them.

Since the goal of Movement for the Mind is to allow the language of creative expression and feelings to emerge in the way most natural to the individual, I sometimes incorporate drawing and stream of consciousness writing (letting thoughts flow without editing) into the debriefing portion of the session. Instead of sharing spoken words, a group shares its drawings and words on paper in small groups. In the creativity workshop at the University of Santa Clara, I incorporated writing and drawing as tools to articulate and integrate their creative experience as dancers, and then added verbal debriefing as a final closure.

Integrating other forms of nonverbal expression with movement seemed to drive home their creative experience. Their words and visual images on paper re-iterated what their choreography spoke through their bodies. Because the movements were not judged, individuals shared that they felt they had permission to accept their creativity whether or not it was perfect or made sense. "I've always thought that in order to be creative, I had to be the perfect dancer and choreographer. Exploring my body freely with movements and then translating my physical moves into images and words, gave me a greater creative range." Another student added, "I never realized how creative just dancing, just moving is. Spending the past two hours immersed in these different art forms, forced me to pay attention to a part of me that I have always tried to ignore, the child in me. I had forgotten how confident and creative this child is."

Although dancers are more familiar with expressing their feelings non-verbally, most of us are accustomed to trying to articulate our feelings intellectually. In some verbal debriefing sections I have watched individuals get over analytical and literally talk their experiences to "death." When I have used writing and drawing as the debriefing session instead of spoken words, the result is often a transformative experience that could not have been achieved merely through talking. It gave people the courage to leap into their creative expression because the boundaries were self-regulating rather then imposed by an intellectual need to understand or analyze. Participants felt that they could be spontaneous and that the nonverbal format supported them in accepting their own experiences without judging or needing to justify the experience. The creative format itself employing dance, music, art, and writing fostered an increase in creative and inspirational potential for each individual. The most common comment in these groups was "It gave me permission to be more spontaneous and to go deeper."

Although integrating different nonverbal art forms may not seem particularly significant, it encourages us to reach beyond the ordinary. Every time we fully embrace our creativity in this way we are inviting new horizons and pushing the edge of what we thought was possible. Statistics show that we may be using only ten per cent of our brain and scientists agree that the actual capabilities of our mind have been barely tapped.[3] Movement for the Mind helps us to loosen the cobwebs of creative inactivity. Creativity invokes dreams, schemes, and greatness. Combining Movement for the Mind with other art forms teaches us how to explore layers of ourselves that linear and rational thinking alone cannot access. It helps us integrate both the right brain

---

[3] Eccles, Sir John. *Neurology Lecture.* Colorado: University of Colorado, July 31, 1994.

and left brain. By using these various forms of art together, it summons the creative child in us to surface. We call forth the unconscious in each of us and open to new perceptual realities. Without this awareness we settle for mediocrity and become reliant on outer things to stimulate and entertain us. Tapping our creative resources banishes boredom and awakens inspiration, hope and the possibility of creative contribution. Today, more than ever, we need imminent and future creative solutions to our global economic, ecological and human dilemmas.

Exercises: Creativity Unbound

Before beginning the physical exercises in this section, pause now and ask yourself these questions, then jot down your answers in your journal. Answering these questions will help increase your level of creative awareness and focus your movement experience.

- How do I define creativity?

- Do I consider myself artistic?

- Do I consider myself creative?

- What do I do to nurture my creative inclinations?

- In what activities do I most connect to my creativity?

- Are these activities mental, emotional, physical, or spiritual?

- How can I enhance my creativity on a daily basis?

To awaken creativity, you must stretch past your safety zone and open to new ways of seeing that go beyond the habitual. You can do the exercises alone or with others. You will want to set aside at least an hour (to two hours) for this session. Think of it as a class that you are taking in the privacy of your own home to help unfold your creative self.

The most important thing to remember is to not to compare yourself to others or to judge yourself or your creation. Let the experience happen inside of you so that your concern is with how you feel and how it expands your perceptual reality. Do not be concerned with controlling the process. This is the time for you to loosen the bonds of systemization, analysis, and restriction. Stay aware of your reactions and your boundaries.

Get drawing paper, crayons, markers or colored pencils as well as your journal. If you paint, feel free to use canvas or watercolor paper and paint. Put the art supplies and your journal to the side of the room.

Before you begin the session survey your room and make sure you have the privacy and space that you need without bumping into anything. Any room will do as long as you can stretch out and take several large steps in all directions. Take off your shoes, place them out of your way and then leave your voice of judgment with your shoes. Read the entire section through once and then you may want to record the instructions to give yourself time to complete each task.

Musical Selections: I will suggest different selections of music, but feel free to choose your own. Remember that music is a motivator, it can support the environment that you are creating or it can work against it like a distraction. There are four sections in this session. We will start with movement and then go to drawing. We will return to moving and then end the session with writing. You can choose different pieces of music for each section or stay with one selection that is both varied and inspirational to you. Some suggestions are: *Bones* by Gabrielle Roth and The Mirrors, *Shamanic Dream, Thunder Drums* by Scott Fitzgerald, *Light Rain/Dark Fire, Passion* by Peter Gabriel. Everyone is inspired by different beats, rhythms, and tones. Choose something that awakens and enlivens you and also allows you the space to be reflective.

Breathing

Find a spot in the room that you feel comfortable in and have the physical dimensions to move in all directions without bumping into anything. Lie down on your back with your feet straight in front of you and your arms comfortably by your side. Close your eyes.

Begin now by taking some deep complete breaths the way you were instructed in Chapter Two for at least five rounds and then allow the natural rhythm of your breath to return. Just observe the natural rhythm of your breath for another five rounds. Allow this natural flow of the in breath and the out breath to be the gage for the rhythm in your movement patterns.

Boundaries

Become aware of your physical boundaries. You will define your physical boundaries through the skin on the surface of your body, which differentiates you from the floor, the air, the music and even the instructions in this section. Touch your skin with your hands so that you know where your body's surface begins and ends. Make sure there's no place on your skin that is numb or undefined where you can disassociate from your body. Take as long as you need to identify your outer boundaries thoroughly. (Pause)

Once you have defined your physical boundaries, mentally go inside your skin and make the space on the inside as spacious and secure as you can conceive. There should be no feelings of restriction here. These are your inner boundaries. It is on the inside that you can safely house your memories, feelings, dreams, images and inner child. No one can judge, change or invalidate this place within your outer boundaries.

Physical, Mental, Emotional, and Spiritual Inventory

Now be aware of your physical body. Notice any heat or cold, comfort or discomfort. Be aware of your energy level. Do you feel tired or invigorated? Do not feel like you have to change anything. Just observe your physical body without judgment for thirty seconds to a minute. Change your focus to your mental state. Is your mind quiet or full of chatter? What is the quality of your thoughts? Simply observe your mental state for about thirty seconds. Now check in with your emotional state. What feelings are available to you right now? Sadness? Joy? Anger? Numbness? Neutrality? Without judging just notice what you feel. Last but not least, become aware of the witness. It is the part of you that no matter what you have gone through is always OK. It is the knower in you who remembers your dreams. You may also call this part source, spirit, or soul. Locate the witness somewhere in your physical body. You may find it in your heart, solar plexus, or anywhere else.

Section I: Physical Doodling

You'll want to first warm up using the Dance Principles and Creative Exploration exercises described on pages 37-41 of Chapter Two for about ten minutes. You can do an abbreviated version of these exercises, but make sure you have moved all the parts of your body and explored the room on all three levels, in four directions, and played with fast and slow tempos. Your body should feel warm and ready for doodling. Feel free to keep your eyes closed unless you are moving physically around the room. You will find it easier to image and feel things with your eyes closed, but please open them when you need to for physical safety.

You are going to begin moving through different visual environments adding various textures, colors, and emotional qualities to your movements. Spend about one minute exploring each different quality.

- Imagine that your entire room is filled with taffy. Move on all levels, in any direction through this sticky stuff. Even the air feels thick. How do you legs, arms, and torso move through taffy?

- Now let the room fill up with sand. Walk on it; move through it; feel the texture against your skin. Soft, grainy, cool or hot feel your body ploughing through it and creating sand sculptures.

- Change the room into velvet. Feel how smooth each of your movements are. Let each leg lift and turn of you torso reflect this rich, silky material. How does this change your mood?

- The environment shifts into concrete. Every time you move you get blocked with this hard slab. It feels cold, hard, and rigid. Keep moving anyway.

- Finally the room fills up with water. First it's freezing cold and just as quickly it turns piping hot. Almost immediately afterwards, it changes to tepid. The water is a perfect temperature, not too hot, not too cold. Feel how it yields to your every movement. Notice how different it feels compared to concrete.

Let the water dissolve and continue moving in any kind of environment that you choose. Listening to the following words, allow them to affect your movements. Think of all the ways each word stimulates you. Let the physical responses to each word last about twenty seconds:

Burst...Wiggle...Crumble...Undulate...Swing...Sizzle...Stagger... Jiggle...Swoop...

Sparkle. Let go and again move in any environment, on any level with whatever thoughts motivate your movements.

Now add color and mood. Explore each one for about a minute. Move as if you were the color of the sun, a deep, glowing, golden yellow. Add the emotional equivalent of this brilliant yellow to your movements. Allow your imagination and your body to run with yellow.

The color changes to a soft blue, like the sky. What emotion is stimulated? It may simply feel peaceful. Or it may summon feelings of sadness. Move with the quality that comes to you.

Now everything turns to black. Add an emotion. You may respond differently to the color black than others. Go with your initial reaction. Keep moving.

Shift to the color red: hot, scintillating, and bright. Add a corresponding feeling. Is it passion, anger or something entirely different? If you start feeling more then one emotion let it come forward through your movements. Remember there is no right or wrong way to move or feel. Allow yourself to be spontaneous. Pick one more color of your choice and create the corresponding emotion. Dance for another minute.

Section II: Creating

Let go of this last color and emotion from your movements and begin to create a dance that represents your next step of personal growth. It may be in any area of your life. For example it could be in the arena of relationships, career, recreation, health, body image or it could relate to something spiritual. It can be any aspect of your life that needs expansion, change, or renewal.

Create from the qualities we just explored. Each environment, texture, color, and emotional quality can be expounded. You want to use your doodling to create a form that moves and expands. The movements may repeat or they may change continuously. If you find yourself repeating certain movement patterns you may try them on different levels or in different directions. You can change your tempo or your rhythm. Each of these changes will add variety and depth to your movements. Like a choreographer you are building on a theme. Continue moving for about ten minutes.

Section III: Bringing the Creation to Paper and Canvas

Slowly bring your movements to a closure. Whether you are standing, sitting or lying down, take a few minutes to just observe your breath. Let your dance move inwardly to the pulse of your breathing. When you feel grounded and complete, open your eyes and get your art supplies out.

Before you start drawing or painting close your eyes again. Visualize the process you just went through. Concentrate on your dance. See the movements, textures, colors, and shapes that symbolically embody the renewal and changes in your life. Now draw or paint the experience of your dance and the meaning behind it. Allow the colors, shapes, and textures to be transferred to paper. Don't worry about being literal. Let the energy move through your hands now the way it moved through your body earlier. New images may surface. Let them. Do not censor anything. Be completely open to yourself and this creation. Take anywhere from ten to twenty minutes for this section.

Section IV: Back to Movement

When you have completed your artwork, take a few minutes to just observe it. Notice the movement of the whole piece and also pay attention to the details. Is there anything familiar about it? What feels new or different to you about this piece? Is there more freedom or more form?

Then step away from it. Close your eyes and begin dancing. Repeat the movement patterns that you created before the artwork. Now let your painting or drawing impact your dance. Embody the colors shapes, textures, and patterns that you translated to paper and completely immerse yourself in the energetic and symbolic merging of dance and art through your body. The music that you have chosen should support this creative expression. Feel free to choose another piece of music if what you originally set aside is no longer appropriate. Continue moving for about ten minutes.

The most important thing to remember is to allow the creative process to unfold. The dance may look and feel completely different then when you first choreographed it. See if you can let your body lead you energetically rather then having to figure it out with your mind.

Inventory

Bring your movements to a closure again by closing your eyes and by becoming aware of the natural rhythm of your breath. You may lie back down on the floor, sit or remain standing.

Repeat the inventory that you did at the beginning of the session. Be aware of your physical body. Notice if you feel differently than when you started. How? What are the sensations in your body? (Pause) Now check in with your mental state. Is your mind quiet? What are the qualities of your thoughts? How is your mental state different then earlier? (Pause) Move on to your emotional state. Observe the colors in your emotional palette. Are there more feelings available to you now? What are they? (Pause) Then once again identify with the witness. Locate it physically and feel the part of you that is connected to spirit and to your source of knowledge. Take a couple of minutes to do this inventory mentally without judgment, and then return to observing your breath for a few more minutes.

Journaling

Feeling fully grounded in your body, with your boundaries intact, gently sit up and get your journal and pen. Begin to write. Let your hand just flow. Don't censor anything. Write your impressions, how you feel, what your dance meant, how your body feels, talk about your art work, describe your next step, what needs changing, etc. Just write. Don't worry about grammar or repetition. You may start out in prose and change to poetry. Or you may simply ramble. Do not strain. Write for at least ten minutes.

Closure

End the session by standing. Close your eyes and feel the floor under your feet. Spend a moment in quiet reflection about this extraordinary creative adventure you have just participated in and unfolded. Let this experience impact the rest of your day and allow it to blossom like a plant inside of you.

Points to Remember

After completing this session you may want to review your answers to the questions asked at the beginning of the exercise. Your perception of your own creativity may have changed. Perhaps it has strengthened your beliefs. Remember to stay open to your own creative unfoldment.

You can repeat the session once a week, once a month or as often as you have time. Each repetition will activate your creativity and give you an opportunity to discover additional perspectives and experiences. Be open to letting the session offer you something new each time you do it. You can vary the music and choose different aspects of your life to clarify and change. Remember to have fun and to invite the child within you to participate.

You may also want to share these Creativity Unbound exercises with your friends or children. Feel free to integrate the principles on brainstorming and team building at work. Applying and expressing what you have learned opens up the possibility for new dialogues and avenues of communication.

For some people, these exercises will activate a part of themselves that they didn't know existed. Others may simply feel a joyous sense of freedom. You may even experience some frustration if your voice of judgment gets activated and you have a tendency to be a perfectionist. There is no wrong or bad response. The purpose of each section of the Creativity Unbound session is to activate your creativity and to bring you closer to the many gifts that lie within you.

Chapter Five:
Dance as Psychotherapy

"We are all dancers. We use movement to express ourselves —
our hungers, pains, angers, joys, confusion, fears —
long before we use words, and we understand the meaning
of movements long before we understand those of words."
— *Franklin Stevens*

Phyllis, a friend of Jane's, called me because she had been battling a weight problem for years and also over ate when she felt under stress. She was in her mid-thirties, a successful attorney, happily married, and the mother of two children.

At first glance, her weight problem did not seem significant. She was articulate about what she wanted and in the first session gave me a brief overview of her life. She was born in Europe and came to the United States with her mother after her parents divorced when she was seven. She had been in therapy for a couple of years and was aware of some painful memories from childhood, but for the most part, she was satisfied with her life.

After the first couple of Movement for the Mind sessions, Phyllis discovered that she had built a wall that prevented her from getting too close to anyone or to experiencing her feelings. She shared, "My God. Feelings are in the body. I can see how my eating is a way to stuff my feelings. In therapy I can talk about things, but I don't have to feel. I never realized how overwhelmed I get by these feelings and what I've done to avoid them." In the ensuing sessions, she discovered that her overeating and symptoms of stress were masking the deeper layers of discomfort that she had hidden since childhood. Although, it was uncomfortable to bring up painful, unfinished business from the past, she realized that not dealing with these issues was costing her intimacy in her marriage, in her friendships, and with her children, and it was keeping her locked up emotionally on the inside.

Movement for the Mind brought these memories to surface and encouraged her to find more appropriate ways of dealing with her feelings as an adult. It allowed her to dislodge her fears about confronting these wounds and to be free in the places that she had previously only covered up and avoided.

Phyllis's story, while unique, is also very common. Wounds and emotionally charged unfinished business from the past often bleed into our present and future circumstances. Out of the numerous clients who have sought help through Movement for the Mind, most of them were not aware of the significance of these dormant issues and the negative impact it was making in their lives. These clients often came complaining about circumstances in their life that had to do with present time issues — such as weight problems, depression, relationship problems, work related issues, or sometimes just a vague feeling of discomfort in the body. Coming from all walks of life, some were severely abused as children and others just experienced the "normal" traumas of growing up. Yet, whether the trauma was severe or moderate, and whether they had conscious memories of these events or not, the unresolved feelings from the past were still affecting their present-day psyche and lives.

In this chapter, we will look at how Movement for the Mind can be used as a path towards psychological wholeness. Although it can be used for any kind of therapy, this chapter will deal primarily with current issues that stem from unresolved traumas from the past through the personal stories of six individuals. While events may occur throughout our lives that cause us to seek therapy, childhood wounds and beliefs often continue to influence our reactions and ways of handling the present until we resolve them consciously.

Movement for the Mind utilizes six steps in the process of psychological healing. These steps may occur simultaneously or in stages depending upon each individual's experience. They are: safely and freely expressing feelings in the body, making the body safe, creating new boundaries that positively influence relationships with others, triggering new emotions that are responsible for changing behavioral patterns, embodying the connection between body, mind, emotions, and spirit, and re-establishing joy, safety and comfort in the body. In addition, in this chapter we will focus on understanding the interrelationship of the psyche and the body and the role of the body in holding and processing memories of trauma.

Interrelationship of Body and Psyche in Treating Trauma

The most significant aspect of Movement for the Mind is also what distinguishes it from talk therapy or any other purely mental approach: the role that the body plays in changing behavior. In Movement for the Mind, the body acts as a conduit for experiencing inner and outer congruity.

Although psychiatrists and many behavioral modification researchers would agree that the key to changing behavior lies in changing one's mental state and belief system, behavioral shifts are not likely to occur unless one creates a congruity between thoughts and feelings. It is the difference between merely wishing for one's fears of abandonment to disappear, and the experience of not panicking in the face of loss while maintaining a physical state of equilibrium. The first only engages the mind, while the second involves an actual shift that occurs mentally, emotionally, and physically.

This act of congruity between the mind and emotions is what occurs in the process of dancing. Engaging the body creatively while physically expressing thoughts and feelings integrates the mental and emotional state. The mind and emotions are united through the body's chemistry. Movement becomes the pipeline that carries the transmission of new emotional signals to the brain. Movement for the Mind integrates the body and mind into a therapy that causes powerful and easily adaptable changes.

Movement for the Mind engages many of the senses in a directed manner. Although, the thematic structure is facilitated, each individual unfolds the creative process uniquely. Words facilitate the process and help to communicate results, but the experience happens between words and continues to impact each person's life at the most basic kinesthetic level. It is a physical repatterning that is birthed out of creatively accessing all of oneself. When one moves, a process of creation takes place that is both embodied and that can be felt, moved, and referred back to physically. New images of support, stability, safety, and worthiness are seeded with each movement pattern deliberately and consciously.

Because Movement for the Mind utilizes a physical, mental, emotional, and spiritual approach, it also encourages the experience of integration, which is essential to psychological healing. Not only are the mind, emotions, and body integrated, but something is also engaged at a deeply spiritual level. When one experiences trauma as a child emotionally, sexually, or physically, a very basic trust in the universal good, in God, or whatever one chooses to call that greater sense of belonging gets shattered. Often that mistrust is transferred to relationships with others as an adult. That schism must be bridged in the body, not just the mind.

For the individuals whose stories I tell here, Movement for the Mind was used as a tool to access and express feelings in the body that had been held back and lay dormant. As the feelings of shame, anger, sadness, pain, and grief were expressed non-verbally and allowed the freedom to "dance" without judgment or censorship, new beliefs, feelings, and patterns could be chosen. In the letting go process, nothing needed to be hidden or to be seen as unacceptable. Then instead of stomping out the past as an unnecessary evil, it was turned into compost, a fertile ground for new seeds to blossom. Releasing the shadows and transforming the dark places into conscious awareness made room for filling in the places that didn't get met emotionally and physically. These individuals were able to create a safe "home" within themselves, to reclaim appropriate boundaries, and to learn how to regain trust. Movement was a language that came naturally to them as it does with most people.

As children, we believe that what adults tells us about ourselves and what they do to us, is a direct statement of who and what we are. We define ourselves largely by the feedback we get outside ourselves. These individuals learned to redefine the term "responsibility." They had no conscious control over their parents, over the events that happened to them, or how they forged their belief systems as children. But they could take responsibility for righting the wrongs inside themselves as adults. They were responsible for their healing and for lifting the veils of false programming.

The stories in this chapter dramatically reflect the capacity that each one of us has to heal wounds from our past and to make profound changes that can positively impact our lives. You can use the information in this chapter and the exercises that follow to change or modify unwanted behaviors, express feelings, or simply to experience your emotions and body more authentically and joyously.

The Role of the Body in Holding and Processing Memories of Trauma

In my clinical work and research, I discovered some studies that seemed to support and clarify why dance and specifically Movement for the Mind is so successful as a therapeutic medium.

One of these studies conducted with Vietnam War Veterans suffering from Post Traumatic Stress Disorder (PTSD) illustrates why Movement for the Mind can play such an effective role both in retrieving memories and in resolving their negative impact.

In a study done with combat Vietnam War Veterans in 1991 by Eugene G. Peniston and Paul J. Kulkosky, alpha-theta brain wave neuro-feedback therapy (BWNT) was substituted for traditional medical treatment with those combat veterans suffering from PTSD. Alpha-theta brain wave training was developed in the late 1960's by biofeedback pioneers Joe Kamiya, Barbara Brown, Elmer Green, and Alyce Green. PTSD is defined by on-going symptoms of anxiety, sleep disorders, alcohol or drug abuse, suicidal thoughts, and depression as a result of highly stressful events. In a four year study Peniston and Kulkosky found unanimously that the application of alpha-theta brain wave training was more effective in the treatment of PTSD, and in the prevention of relapses then traditional modalities of treatment.[4]

I learned about this study from Dr. Steven Stockdale who practices in Colorado and specializes in diagnostic evaluations and neuro-feedback training for patients with a number of conditions including attention deficit disorders, PTSD, and disorders of anxiety, depression, and alcoholism. Stockdale suggested that my Movement for the Mind work with clients who had experienced child abuse had similarities to the BWNT results with war veterans.

In alpha-theta brain wave training, participants learn to access brain waves that are associated with deep states of relaxation and with creative, nonverbal, and non-linear states. This differs from normal waking state activity where adults primarily function in a beta brain wave state. Beta brain wave patterns are most associated with the intellect and are produced when processing information, thinking, concentrating, and learning. Beta brain wave patterns occur when we are using our mind to think rationally and analytically.

[4] Kulkosky, Paul & Peniston, Eugene. Alpha-Theta Brainwave Neuro-Feedback For Vietnam Veterans With Combat-Related Post Traumatic Stress Disorder. Toronto: Hogrefe & Huber Publishers, 1991.

In contrast, children produce primary frequencies in alpha and theta. The beta state develops more with age and maturation. Stockdale stated, "one could hypothesize that children who are victims of abuse receive that trauma when their brain's primary electro physiological pattern is in the slower frequencies (alpha and theta). Since these experiences and memories are often repressed, using alpha-theta brainwave training in adults who experienced trauma as children could facilitate the recall of such information and be useful in the healing process."

In the study with the Vietnam War Veterans, a therapist helped them facilitate and process the imagery and information from their brain wave therapy training sessions, and they were able to resolve the symptoms and effects of their Post Traumatic Stress. Dr. Stockdale added, "Other creative nonverbal activities and therapies such as dance/movement and guided imagery could also access the alpha-theta brainwave state and produce the same satisfactory results. Since survivors of any severe childhood trauma often exhibit similar symptoms as combat war veterans diagnosed with PTSD, activities that facilitate the alpha-theta brain wave state could also be highly effective in treating survivors of childhood abuse."

Re-Accessing the State of the Child

These theories led me to examine the idea that in treating traumas from childhood, we need to re-access the state of the child not the adult. It is the child who holds the key to the memories, beliefs, and feelings that have caused so much distress.

The effects of a trauma do not necessarily stop with the cessation of the event. Frequently, beliefs evolve as a result of the trauma, and these beliefs carry forth a life of their own like a self fulfilling prophecy. The mind may completely blot out the memory, but the body seems to remember. If there has been no resolution or emotional expression allowed at the time of the trauma, which is so often the case for children, then these feelings are repressed and frozen in the body.

The child is affected on all levels and the affects usually do not go away by growing up into an adult. The coping and survival behaviors adopted by children often lead to undesirable and inappropriate acts by adults. It is the adult who may seek therapy, but it is the child who is crying out. Traditional therapy can address the belief system and is often a comfortable medium for the adult who now primarily communicates through the intellect and words. But words cannot touch the core of the trauma or abuse.

A child does all of his/her explorations from the body. Instincts such as eating, sleeping, and sensing fear are tied to the body. As a child grows and develops the mind, intellect, feelings, and spirit are housed within the body. Yet, the most powerful language of all, dance, the language of the body, is rarely and then only intermittently and unconventionally used in therapy.

Movement for the Mind activates the alpha-theta state, the brain wave state of the child, whose wounds are at the core of the adult's present problems. The memories, beliefs and behavioral patterns issue from this "inner child." It is by activating and addressing the inner child's core beliefs, memories, and feelings that actual healing can take place.

Byron's Story

Byron was a tall attractive man in his early forties. His was big and muscular, but his voice was very quiet and soft, almost melodious, and also very monotone. His persona was that of a big teddy bear, a really nice, agreeable guy. Although he was in therapy, he confided, "I don't know how to express my feelings." In our first consultation he told me that he felt completely disconnected from his inner child and his emotions. "I don't know how to express anger, but I think I have a lot of rage in me," he continued.

He then told me that he had recently divorced his wife. Their relationship had lacked physical and emotional intimacy throughout their fifteen-year marriage. The only intimacy and love that he allowed himself to feel was through sex with prostitutes. After finally ending a relationship with a prostitute who was also a cocaine addict, he sought help in therapy.

During that first session he told me that he had very few memories of his childhood, and yet somehow he knew he had to reclaim that lost part of himself. He was an accountant and did not consider himself artistic. He had never taken a dance class or worked with creative movement in any capacity before, but he was willing to try anything that could help unleash this hidden part of himself. He agreed to come to a weekly one hour Movement for the Mind group class in addition to weekly private sessions. He also continued seeing his regular therapist.

From the very first class, he adopted his own unique style for moving. He was very rhythmic and engaged his upper body in large swinging flow patterns. Each movement session (both the class and private work) was preceded and concluded with verbal sharing. Byron was never at a loss for movement, but when it came time to translate his experience into words, he could not articulate it. We agreed that the goal was to free his feelings and that the by-product was the intellectual understanding. Words and analysis could come later.

Slowly "little Byron" began to emerge. During a private Movement for the Mind session using guided imagery, he reclaimed a memory when he was five years old. He had come home from school crying and his mother was furious with him for crying and carrying on. She never asked him why he was crying, instead he was carried into an ice cold shower, fully clothed, and forced to remain there until he stopped crying. Repeatedly, incidents occurred that shut down his feelings until there was nothing left to little Byron except outer obedience and complacency. Secretly, he would take his hurt and anger out on animals, torturing frogs and cats while his own voice remained silent.

For the first time since he was five years old, Byron began to re-experience the feelings that were denied to him for most of his life. I used his own images to guide him through a process where the five year old could safely express his feelings through Byron's body. Non-verbally, little Byron began to reveal himself. The terror that he had been subject to also gave way to other emotions. Kinesthetically he touched sadness, rage, abandonment, and grief.

The more that Byron allowed his inner child, especially the wounded and split off part of himself, to kinesthetically express and move, the more Byron realized that he was not to blame for his mother's emotional abuse. As Byron danced and created movement patterns through a guided format, he regained a voice that had been shut down for over thirty-five years.

Building Appropriate Boundaries

Because his accumulative childhood experiences contributed to the fragmentation of his emotional self from his physical self, I worked with Byron on boundaries. I helped him define his own physical boundaries through the awareness of his skin's surface. This physical awareness of where his skin began and ended, distinguished him from the floor, air, and even my voice. Then, I had Byron locate his inner boundaries by creating a spatial awareness inside his body. That "space" on the inside of the skin's surface could be as limitless and expansive as he desired. It was also a place of safety and security where his feelings and memories could be housed and expressed. I had Byron move in the awareness of these new boundaries and then invited little Byron into his inner boundaries.

Byron developed a great deal of love and respect for this neglected and wounded child within himself. But anger was still difficult for Byron to fully express. He was terrified that if he let go, he would go out of control like a volcano destroying everything in its path. I often used a portion of Peter Gabriel's Passion, to set the environmental mood for these sessions. But it never worked to directly address anger.

Instead, Byron's process was wonderfully organic and a reminder that you can't rush or force the healing process. Over time, as he unveiled his memories in therapy, through our work and by journaling, Byron got closer to bridging the emotional gap within himself. After continuing in this way, using Movement for the Mind to dance the images, feelings, and memories, Byron had his breakthrough that he had been longing for.

It came in a group therapy workshop in the early morning hours. He screamed, pounded pillows, ripped phone books to shreds and allowed the raging damned up waters to flow without hurting himself or anyone else. The five year old had broken the emotional silence permanently, and there was no turning back.

This was not the end of Byron's work, but it was a major turning point. In another therapy workshop, he came to the workshop prepared to confront his mother. He built a doll-like life size replica of her and brought it with him. When it was his turn to work, he let the doll have it verbally and tore her down physically and symbolically. But what followed no one anticipated. Within her doll-like structure he had buried a treasure chest full of items from his re-created childhood. Out tumbled stuffed animals, baby booties, beautifully framed photos of little Byron, rubber duckies and a silver, heart shaped bowl filled with semi-precious stones! Out of a tragically repressive and abusive past, Byron had reclaimed his own self-worth as a child and as an adult. Byron creatively re-scripted his past and took back what had been stolen. He moved with a new found pride in his body that spoke of authenticity and joy.

Working from the Inside-Out

Byron taught me the importance of not having to make it happen. Even as therapists, it's so easy to want to fix our clients or control their healing process. Byron reiterated the small still voice within myself that said to trust his process. I could have used traditional dance therapy methods to help him change his movement patterns or to make his voice match more authentically what he said he was feeling. Instead, we worked from the inside out, first by expanding his language of expression through movement and then by connecting to his inner child. He had the courage to face his inner pain and wounds and that led him to a wonderfully creative and magical part of himself.

The inner work naturally spilled over to his daily life transforming his relationships and his attitudes. He ended relationships that were no longer healthy emotionally for him and was able to communicate his needs while still expressing compassion and concern for others. He had released his shame and replaced it with self-respect. Physically there were also changes. His voice had more range and was no longer monotone. He had successfully integrated his inner child and had adopted clear boundaries. He knew when our work was complete and he terminated his therapy with the same clarity. He continued with Movement for the Mind classes and knew that his creativity was now a moving, breathing part of his self. Life still had its challenges, but he had triumphed in the broken places. No one could take that inner integration away from him again.

Connecting the Emotional Body

Thinking or talking about something cannot replace the act of feeling. When Byron first described his anger towards his mother, he spoke in soft harmonious tones. He was talking about his reaction, but there was no emotional connection. For Byron that emotional connection was essential to his healing. We used talking to clarify events and to establish intellectual understanding, but most of the work was designed to unleash the feelings of the past. I used verbal cues and guided imagery in a similar fashion as one would use in basic hypnosis or any other format of guided imagery. But that was only the stepping stone for working with the body.

I incorporated music to more fully engage the senses. Using all of these elements created a synthesis of mental, emotional, and physical stimulation — one that was experienced inside Byron's body. After these sessions I would encourage Byron to write, either by using his non dominant hand as is suggested in Lucia Capaccione's book, *The Power Of Your Other Hand,* or by writing in a continuous stream of consciousness. All of these tools worked together to forge an inner connection which he had lost sight of as a child. But the main spoke of the recovery wheel was Movement for the Mind. It is in the dance that he reclaimed memories, expressed feelings, and unraveled old limiting beliefs and replaced them with new ones.

Frank's Story: Transforming Pain into Power

Frank called me after reading a newspaper article featuring my work on Movement for the Mind. "I am not in touch with my feelings and I also don't feel connected to my body," he said to me on the telephone. After exchanging information about my work, he asked if he could make an appointment to see me.

When he entered my office, I noticed that both his physical appearance and his mannerisms were more feminine than masculine. His physique was round and soft, his hair was overgrown around his ears, and he was gentle and soft spoken. Frank was an engineer in his early fifties and had been married and divorced twice. He confided that in both relationships he had been the caretaker.

As he began to tell me about his family and his past, a picture began to unfold. "My father is in prison for life. My mother had a nervous breakdown after thirty years of marriage and never recovered. My brother is homeless. One sister is in a mental institution, another is an alcoholic, and my other sister is on welfare. All my life, I felt like I had to take care of my mother and protect my siblings."

His father was among other things a bully and a rageaholic. He had little patience with Frank as a child and whenever Frank was asked to do a task, his father abruptly took the project away from him, telling Frank that he was too slow and couldn't do anything right.

Frank had consciously made a decision while growing up to be nothing like his father. Showing aggression, force, or anger was not an option for Frank. But neither was sadness, grief, joy, or exuberance. He chose instead to bury his needs and to take care of others. He had survived his childhood with a measure of sanity and had escaped substance abuse and other self-destructive behaviors that enveloped the rest of his siblings.

As we began to explore his past through conversation, guided imagery, and movement, Frank began to see that the issues he was having at work and with others stemmed from patterns established in childhood. We recreated each stage of childhood in his body allowing his responses and feelings to emerge and to be danced and expressed through the use of the Dance Principles and guided imagery. Because Frank was so willing to feel what had been glossed over in his childhood, including the uncomfortable emotions of anger, sadness, and grief he was free to change their impact. He realized that by feeling anger and other strong emotions he did not need to become violent and abusive like his father. We worked instead to turn these emotions into strengths.

In numerous sessions we concentrated on grounding, allowing Frank to actually feel the strength and power in his abdomen, legs, and feet. He noticed that he had always glided while he walked, his feet barely touching the ground. He began to experiment with a gait that made him feel more solid physically and emotionally. Each session built on the previous one bringing a clearer perception of what was unfinished from the past and what could be changed and realized in the present.

His physical appearance began to change. One day he walked in with his hair cut and shaped. He bought a new wardrobe of clothes and began to take greater pride in his appearance. He was still gentle and soft spoken, but now he radiated a definite male essence. "It never felt safe identifying with my masculinity before," he realized, "I always hated what my father stood for and if that meant being a male, I didn't want to have anything to do with it."

His self-esteem improved. He was able to break negative work habits that he had unconsciously scripted from childhood, and he entered into a healthy relationship with a woman who he felt was his equal. He also began to engage in creative activities that he had been reluctant to participate in previously.

In both Byron's and Frank's stories, we see examples of how Movement for the Mind consciously paves the way for positive physical, emotional, and mental changes. Repressed feelings and negative behavioral patterns are transformed into present life affirming choices. In the following pages we will look at the significance and meaning of experiencing the body as safe.

Making the Body Safe

I was asked to give a series of workshops for therapists and therapy interns at Parents United in San Jose, California. One of the topics I chose was "Patterns Born of Sexual Abuse."

From my own experience as an incest survivor and as someone who has worked with many hundreds of other survivors, I have found that the dominant theme is that the body is not perceived as safe. As humans our bodies are our homes. Our thoughts, feelings and actions are communicated through our bodies. Quite literally without bodies we wouldn't be here.

Not feeling safe in the body carries life-altering significance. When children are reared in unsafe homes and neighborhoods plagued with drugs and violence, we are alerted to the life threatening consequences. When the home we occupy twenty four hours a day is experienced as unsafe the situation may be hidden, but the threats are not all that different. Many patterns born of sexual abuse stem from the constant stress of feeling unsafe in the body.

Ultimately, this feeling can create low self-esteem, eating disorders, chemical dependencies, obsessive behaviors, disassociation, multiple personalities, suicide attempts, depression, intimacy dysfunctions, and health problems. These symptoms similar to PTSD are like behavioral maps that keep the abuse and unresolved feelings alive in the body. They are the unconscious memories and feelings frozen in physical tendencies that can affect every area of an individual's life. These patterns arise from a complex interplay of action and reaction and invoke responses that involve the mind, body, emotions, and spirit. Being unsafe in the body creates a constant need to escape, numb, block out, or repeat the only thing known.

Terrie's Story

Terrie was in her mid-twenties and had spent the last four years traveling around Europe and the United States. She was living on a trust fund left to her by her grandfather and spent her time pursuing creative and self-actualization ventures. She had dated a few men, but had never experienced a long term committed relationship. About a year previous to our work she became aware of a growing uneasiness in her body. She had few conscious memories about her childhood, just this uneasiness that she could not shake, an inability to commit to a job, relationship or home for more then a few months, and a general fear and obsessiveness about her body and men.

"I know that I hold all my tension in my stomach," she said, "and I don't feel real good about my body or my weight. It's something I obsess about all the time."

From the very first session, the feelings of being unsafe in her body became apparent. As we began to explore her earliest memories of these feelings through movement, music, and guided imagery, a seven year story unfolded. She began to remember the sexual acts with her grandfather. Her earliest memories began at the age of six months and continued until the age of seven. Two cousins who confessed that they had remembered being molested by this grandfather before she ever shared her story later confirmed her reclaimed memories and flashbacks.

Ironically, it was the grandfather's business and financial success that provided for the entire family. After his death he provided an outer structure of stability, but inwardly he had shattered the family's foundation. Terrie later learned that her father had also been molested as a child (in foster homes) and that the same grandfather had violated her mother. No one talked about this shared legacy until Terrie confronted her family.

In the beginning, our work was primarily focused on allowing Terrie to feel what had been locked up inside of her since she was a baby. She spent those initial sessions crying and feeling just how uncomfortable it was to stay present in her body. Her dance was awkward and painful, but also filled with compassion for her inner child where previously there had been only shame.

The patterns that Terrie had developed were deeply ingrained. She had trouble separating herself from the unconscious collective beliefs that had been handed down. All of us to a certain extent are given this task of sorting out what has been handed down to us out of ignorance and what is rightfully ours to develop and own. This is part of the natural maturation and self-actualization process, but the act of sexual abuse creates a diffusion of boundaries that makes this task doubly difficult.

Terrie's awareness of not being safe had created a pattern of always making sure she could escape. As a child, she simply disassociated; as an adolescent and adult this behavior developed into a pattern of never sticking with anything long enough to make a commitment. She had learned early on that "Grandpa" would always find her and she was determined to not fall prey to other "grandpas." Unfortunately, her patterns of escape only triggered the discomfort and hidden wounds. At the core of her need to escape was the feeling of being bad and unworthy.

After bringing many of her memories and hidden feelings to a conscious state, and then expressing them fully in the body through Movement for the Mind, Terrie was able to begin to reframe both her self-image and her patterns. In the early stages of our work together she shared, "While dancing I have glimpses of feeling in harmony with my body for the very first time." Her healing was a process that unraveled and then redesigned the pieces of the puzzle.

But the core issue for her was reclaiming the safety of her body. The Movement for the Mind sessions consistently brought her back to a feeling of safety until it replaced the old familiar need to escape. These inner changes were reflected in her life. Terrie found an entry-level job that was in her field of interest and worked her way up into a satisfactory and responsible position. Instead of continually traveling as she had done in the previous four years, she decided to take residence in one city and learned how to positively grow roots for the first time in her life.

Engaging the Body to Transform the Mind

The changes that Byron, Frank, and Terrie were able to make were partially possible because of a process that occurs in Movement for the Mind not unlike Neuro Linguistic Programming (NLP). NLP uses a combination of affirmative statements with visual and mental exercises to reframe experiences of the past. These techniques are intended to lessen and even eliminate the impact of negative associations on present day reality. They are also used to reprogram new beliefs into the present and future. John Bradshaw in his book, Home Coming, refers to the use of NLP specifically mentioning the technique of "anchoring" as a way to re-script one's personal history and childhood experiences.[5]

In using anchors one employs a physical gesture such as pressing the thumb and index finger together to activate new thought patterns about past events. Anchors are generally stimulated through the senses and activate old memories. A negative anchor could be a sound in the middle of the night triggering fear and dread. A positive anchor might be the smell of the ocean activating the memory of playful and joyous vacations by the seashore. By substituting positive images each time a negative association occurs, the mind can reframe a new model. The whole purpose of the technique is to consciously replace traumatic memories with positive and life-affirming thoughts and feelings.

In Movement for the Mind, anchoring takes place through certain movements such as grounding the legs and feet, or through other gestures that create an experience of strength and well-being in the body. New mental images and affirmative statements are combined with movement to create a multidimensional experience. When the whole body is engaged, the mind is receptive to new input. Music, movement, verbal encouragement, and emotional response, all part of Movement for the Mind, allow these new

---

[5] Bradshaw, John. Home Coming New York: Bantam Books, 1990, P.178–187

images to become an integral part of the individual. This is an experience that can be felt and acted out from head to toe; that moves, breathes, and is experienced in the body. It is as real as anything the individual has experienced before both physically and emotionally, and therefore it can be realized.

One of the most powerful parts of the process is taking back control. Feelings can be expressed without harmful consequences and new ones can be chosen. There is nothing more self redeeming for anyone who has experienced betrayal or a lack of control over certain events, then the ability to take back the dignity of one's own feelings and body.

Marie's Story: Building a Bridge Between Mind and Body

Marie had been in therapy for years when she came to see me. She was about fifty pounds overweight and in her mid-thirties. She had never been married and had raised her daughter, who was now a teenager, as a single mother. Although short in stature, she appeared self assured and was very articulate in expressing herself. Outwardly, she was a fierce survivor. She conducted herself in such a way to make sure that no one would get too close. She knew how to assert herself by getting angry and staying detached emotionally, but inwardly she told me, "I feel weak, trapped, and utterly defenseless."

Her Achilles heel was her body. Words were her weapon and intellectually she had broken the silence, reclaimed her memories, and basically felt that she knew as much as her therapists. She also knew that her body was uncharted and very unsafe territory. Analysis was Marie's expertise, so my first assignment with her was to have her feel and move without figuring it all out.

Marie had been molested from the age of five until she was in her teens by a friend of the family who she had been sent to live with while her mother established herself financially. Her second sexual encounter was with the father of her child at the age of sixteen. Her third and most recent sexual involvement was with a man whom she stayed casually active with for about eleven years. She never had a "relationship" with either of these two men. She simply had sex with them. She expected nothing emotionally from them and never experienced the friendship or receprocity that relationships generally offer. It never occurred to her to ask for anything more.

The Movement for the Mind sessions for Marie were immediately translated literally. "What I need in a relationship is space," she announced determinately while we were discussing her relationships. Instead of asking her to elaborate on this subject through words, I had her explore this need for space non-verbally through dance. In that session, she was able to consciously explore a relationship pattern that had been established through her body's automatic response for survival.

As a child, Marie's only reprise from being violated by her molester was when she physically or emotionally removed herself from him. Sometimes she could get away physically and other times she split mentally from her body. Her pattern in relationships, which was to just have sex, and plenty of "space," was initially established as a means of escape. The dance work not only revealed her patterns, but it allowed her to explore feelings that she had previously completely ignored.

As Marie grew older she learned how to protect herself through words and by putting on physical weight. No one was going to get that close to her again. Outwardly she had built a physical, mental, and emotional fortress but on the inside she knew she was lying.

She hated and blamed her little girl and her body. Her inner child was locked in her body and she wanted none of it. The patterns she had developed touched all areas of her life including the way she matured mentally and had cut herself off physically. Her need to escape also extended to the way she handled her finances and other areas of material responsibility. Although, she had the money to pay her bills, she was often late with her payments and developed bad credit as a result.

Marie worked with me for over three years, privately and attending workshops. In that time she unraveled her patterns and established a new congruity with her body. Marie, perhaps more then any other client, taught me about both the power and the frailty of the intellect. Intellectually, Marie was brilliant. She had a grasp and understanding of her past that rivaled psychology textbooks. Her imagination was sharp and she could articulate her feelings and ideas with direct precision. But it took longer for her to connect inwardly to her feelings and to her body, and to make beneficial shifts than other clients whose mental acuity was less developed. Marie used her intellect to survive. Through her mind she could keep people at a distance, but she also held stubbornly to negative beliefs about herself. Movement for the Mind was essential to shifting her mentally restrictive paradigms and outdated negative behavioral patterns.

Marie's task was connecting her mind with her body. But for some individuals the core issue involves the body itself. When someone experiences themselves as ugly or bad, no mirror or external opinion will reflect anything differently until they experience an inner shift. Moreover, their lack of self-esteem is directly linked to their lack of body-esteem. The incongruity between how they view themselves, how others see them, and how they feel inwardly about themselves can impact every area of their life.

Michelle's Story: Experiencing Congruity — Body-Esteem Equals Self-Esteem

When Michelle first showed up at a workshop, she personified all the characteristics of the all American, ideal woman. She was tall, beautiful, intelligent, caring, artistic, and diplomatic. Everything looked perfect on the outside. But within the first hour of the workshop, that outer layer peeled and a different image was revealed. "People are always telling me that I am beautiful and that I look great, but inwardly I feel ugly and unlovable." For Michelle it was the first time that she had admitted these feelings and had allowed the wall to come down.

After the workshop she sent me a narrative poem that she had written in the form of a fairy tale. The story was about a princess who had fallen prey to monsters. When the first monster came to woo the princess he was disguised as a prince, but in reality he was an ogre. The ogre courted her with music that created a spell over her. This spell kept her in a fog. Only by running away could she dispel the fog. The story was about her search for love, companionship, and most of all, trust.

Michelle had been running from real ogres all her life. As a child she was left to care take her younger siblings when her mother physically abandoned them. When the children were separated and sent to foster homes, it was Michelle who fought powerlessly for their unity. Two years later when her mother was reassigned custody, incest became a way of life. The first experience was with Michelle's uncle. When she told her mother what her uncle had done, her mother's reply was, "Oh that happens to all little girls." After that, she was repeatedly violated by her mother's boyfriends. Michelle married and divorced before she was twenty years old, and moved from one relationship to another searching to dispel the fog and to run from the ogres. Outwardly she appeared perfectly content and normal. No one saw through her mask, least of all herself.

It was in the Movement for the Mind sessions that her inner vulnerability began to shine through. At first she was terrified, but as she learned to separate the ugliness that she had been subjected

to from what she believed was a statement about herself, she began
to summon the courage to reveal her true self.

After several months of working together she shared this
profound insight. "Even though people kept telling me how pretty
I was, whenever I looked at myself in the mirror all I could see was
the ugliness that had happened to me. I figured if something so
awful could happen to me, it must mean that I'm ugly and awful. Of
course I had to pretend that I was OK, so people wouldn't find out
what I thought was the truth about me."

Michelle like many of us had carved out a picture that was
acceptable to the world. She resided in a body that had a two-way
mirror that just did not reflect. This picture also helped her to
camouflage the truth about her past and the sordid beliefs that
accompanied the acts that she had been powerless to stop. In a
society that primarily judges who we are by outer appearances,
Michelle had learned to use her physical image to survive.

For Michelle, the Movement for the Mind work was about
reclaiming trust and authenticity, and changing her beliefs about
herself. She looked like she should have had all the body-esteem in
the world, but inwardly she had none. She shared, "My mind could
affirm all kinds of beautiful thoughts, but my body knew no such
reality. It had a cellular programming all its own and it did not feel
beautiful, worthy, loved, or safe and no thoughts, words, or attitude
alone could make a dent in that experience."

Michelle began to realize that trust started in her own body.
The Movement for the Mind sessions allowed her to listen to herself
for the very first time. Dance, because it is crafted by the individual
through the body, is both an unraveling and recreation of the self.
In this creative and nonverbal space, the rigid forms of her world
softened. First the dark places came tumbling forth. As she allowed

what she called her "monsters" expression, something bright also began to seep through. But this time it was real. It was not fabricated by a need to hide the shadow parts.

She discovered that trusting the unknown in her movement patterns in each session was comparable to trusting herself at deeper and deeper levels. Because dance is largely about moving through transitions as in level, direction, rhythmic and tempo changes, the practice of learning how to do this smoothly creates a pragmatic skill. Michelle began to move through the rapid changes occurring in her life with greater ease and was able to ground her self-awareness in her body.

All of these discoveries were not made intellectually; they were made in the process of movement and with each session as feelings that had lain dormant for years were expressed, new associations became possible. The only thing that was discarded was the false beliefs and opinions that had never been hers to begin with.

Probably the greatest triumph for Michelle was in discovering her own self-worth and authenticity. Previously, there had been no place that she could be safe to express her true feelings or personality that wasn't fashioned by the expectations of others.

Her Movement for the Mind experience allowed her to dispel many of the dark myths that she had kept inwardly hidden and to reclaim a joyous aspect of herself that wasn't contingent on the opinion of others.

Natalie's Story: Discovering Safety and Extending it into Relationships

Natalie had twenty reasons why she didn't want to attend a dance workshop. The one that stuck out like a sore thumb was that she was terrified to work with her body. She was not a dancer and moving in her body was something she reluctantly did by rote every day. Her incest memories were just too painful to stay consciously physically connected. And she knew that participating in the workshop meant physical connection. That first day, she barely moved. She spent most of the time just redefining and working with her boundaries.

The following session she arrived half an hour early even though she lived more than an hour away from the location of the workshop. She shared, "I found a freedom and joy in my body that was unlike anything I've ever experienced before and it lasted all week!"

Each session, Natalie regained more trust and began to explore other issues through the dance work. She played out feelings and thoughts that had been touched upon in private therapy.

In most of the sessions, unlike traditional group dance workshops, I emphasized individual expression. The group presence was more background and largely incidental to each person's journey. In one session, however, I included the group energy dynamically. Not only was each participant a socialized and supportive part of the group, but each person became interdependent to the next. We worked in dyads and triads (similar to the format mentioned in Chapter Two) and boundaries were tested while the language of movement expanded past previously held perimeters.

Each person was responsible to herself and to the group. Although this is the social dynamic we're all faced with in our families, at work, in our peer groups, and with our society at large, this exercise provided a different perspective. Natalie and many of the others in the group had learned from childhood to give up herself for the sake of another. This extended to her experience of her physical, mental, and emotional boundaries and was repeated in partnerships and most group interactions. Her body knew no other type of relationship. It was automatic and instinctual. The pattern of isolation, numbing, and intimacy dysfunction was a constant reminder to her of being unsafe with others. Yet, in these Movement for the Mind sessions she had experienced herself and her body differently. In this room she was in control of her body and her feelings.

When the group interaction was added, Natalie's initial response was to re-enact her old pattern. But because she had experienced her body as safe, she also had the capacity to interact in a new way. The Movement for the Mind work in small groups and partnerships forced her to utilize new skills in experiencing herself and her response to others as she shaped a new language of communication, boundary, and connection.

Natalie came out of this workshop fortified. She was able to maintain the safety and integrity of her own body while relating to others. She experimented with giving and receiving, moving towards someone and backing away without disappearing or numbing out. She did this non-verbally and spontaneously. Most importantly, she never compromised herself. The experience she had in this workshop did not go away. It was a breakthrough in relationship patterns that she began to practice differently in her daily life. The changes were her choice and the adaptation came as a result of her inner body awareness.

Because Movement for the Mind first offers individuals safety in the presence of a group, it is easier to feel safe with a partner. The nonverbal medium allows for a testing of boundaries and inter-relatedness based on physical trust. There are no words to mask the initial response or the physical and emotional shifts that may arise spontaneously. Movement for the Mind further allows individuals to act out their feelings and impulses probably for the first time. Giving expression to feelings long buried through a creative modality is an act of physical freedom. Because the movement is self-motivated and generated, it offers a direct physical experience of taking back control of one's body while in relationship to others.

Ultimately Movement for the Mind is about reclaiming one's authenticity and joyous spirit. Expressing painful feelings, retrieving repressed memories, and releasing negative behavioral patterns are merely hard work if they do not produce a worthy outcome — one that can be as profound as a life transformed and as simple as a gift of pure joy.

Exercises: Dance as Psychotherapy

Any of these exercises may be practiced alone or with others. In this chapter the focus will be on you, the individual. If you have the time, you'll want to first warm up with the exercises in Chapter Two. Once you are familiar with the movement vocabulary you can go on to this section. There are two different guided movement sections included in this chapter. You can experience them separately and treat them as individual exercises or you can do them both in one session. Before you begin the sessions survey your room and make sure you have the privacy and space that you need without bumping into anything. Any room will do as long as you can stretch out and take several large steps in all directions. Take off your shoes, place them out of your way and then leave your voice of judgment (VOJ) with your shoes.

After you have completed the exercises, write down the feelings, memories or any other impulses that you may have experienced while moving. You may want to read what you have written out loud several times, but do not strain to intellectually figure out what happened. Allow the experience to remain as physical and emotional as you can, and trust that the insights will be revealed to you in an appropriate and timely manner. The most important point is to let your body do the communicating and to not judge or censor any of the movements or feelings.

Read the entire section through once and then you may want to record the instructions and move to the sound of your own voice pausing in the appropriate places to give yourself time to complete each task.

Section I: The Body is Safe

Musical Selections: Feel free to add music to your sessions. Remember that music is a motivator, it can support the environment that you are creating or it can work against it like a distraction. I recommend "Canon in D" by Johann Pacibel. There are so many wonderful variations available. Choose your favorite. Or if this piece is not available, select any calming piano or violin music that resonates a harmonious sound and feeling to you. We will be moving in this section for about fifteen to twenty minutes.

Breathing

Find a spot in the room that you feel comfortable in and have the physical dimensions to move in all directions without bumping into anything. Lie down on your back with your feet straight in front of you and your arms comfortably by your side. Close your eyes.

Begin now by taking some deep complete breaths the way you were instructed in Chapter Two for at least five rounds and then allow the natural rhythm of your breath to return. Just observe the natural rhythm of your breath for another five rounds. Allow this natural flow of the breath to be the gage for the rhythm in your movement patterns.

Boundaries

Become aware of your physical boundaries. You will define your physical boundaries through the skin on the surface of your body, which differentiates you from the floor, the air, the music, and even the instructions in this section. Touch your skin with your hands so that you know where your body's surface begins and ends. Make sure there's no place on your skin that is numb or undefined where you can disassociate from your body. Take as long as you need to identify your outer boundaries thoroughly. (Pause)

Once you have defined your physical boundaries, mentally go inside your skin and make the space on the inside as spacious and secure as you can conceive. There should be no feeling of restriction here. These are your inner boundaries. It is here that you can safely house your memories, feelings, images and inner child. No one can judge, change or violate this place within your outer boundaries. You no longer need to leave your body to be safe.

Physical, Mental, Emotional, and Spiritual Inventory

Now be aware of your physical body. Notice any heat or cold, comfort or discomfort. Be aware of your energy level. Do you feel tired or invigorated? Do not feel like you have to change anything. Just observe your physical body without judgment for thirty seconds. Change your focus to your mental state. Is your mind quiet or full of chatter? What is the quality of your thoughts? Simply observe your mental state for about thirty seconds. Now check in with your emotional state. What feelings are available to you right now? Sadness? Joy? Anger? Numbness? Neutrality? Without judging, just notice what you feel. Last but not least become aware of the witness. It is the part of you that no matter what you have gone through is always OK. It is the knower in you who remembers your dreams. You may also call this part source, spirit, or soul. Locate the witness somewhere in your physical body. You may find it in your heart, solar plexus, or anywhere else.

After you have warmed up with the Movement Vocabulary in Chapter Two and feel ready to proceed, close your eyes again. You may be sitting, standing, or lying down. Recall the first time you felt unsafe or uncomfortable in your body. You may remember a specific incident as an adult or you may catch a glimpse of yourself as a child. If it is an image, a distinct memory, or merely a vague sensation, allow yourself to bring it fully to mind now. Watch as you recall this feeling and allow it to fully come alive in your physical body. What is your initial response? Do you split? Does your stomach tie up in knots?

Take the time now to go deeper into your physical body until all that is left is this experience of being uncomfortable or unsafe. Begin to move physically, allowing this part of you complete expression. Let this aspect that tends to escape have its dance. Notice if it is small or large. Is it tight and dark, or is it slithery and loose? Listen to the music and notice its calming influence. Know that no matter how unsafe the feelings expressed in this dance are, the environment is now safe. You are separate from the initial experience. You are just allowing, maybe for the first time, the expression of these feelings. Continue dancing. Use any level, direction, tempo or energy flow that feels natural. Let your body do the feeling and the moving. Continue for about five to seven minutes.

As your movement comes to an end, release the unsafe feelings. Feel yourself physically placing them outside of your body. Let them go, while remaining grounded and aware of your physical boundaries. To do this, take some deep breaths and as you consciously reframe your physical boundaries, imagining these unsafe feelings outside of yourself.

Now become aware of your inner boundaries and re-establish them as safe and secure. Begin moving with the awareness of your inner and outer boundaries foremost in your mind. Using the *Dance Principles,* move around the room. As you vary your movements, vigilantly maintain your boundaries. You may need to open your eyes as you move around the room. Be aware of your breath and your center of gravity. Let all your movements be motivated out of this inner place of safety.

Feel what it's like to move low to the ground, to move while kneeling, and while standing on half toe. Move deliberately fast or slow. Use staccato or smooth, long, rhythms. Move backward, forward, or sideways. With each step or spatial dynamic know where you physically begin and end. Stay in your skin. Retain this awareness of your boundaries.

Now add emotional tones to your movements. You may want to work with qualities such as strength and weakness, assertiveness and shyness. Or you may want to emulate powerful emotions such as anger, despair, fear, confusion, sadness, or joy. Whatever emotional qualities you begin to add to your movement flows, maintain contact with your boundaries and your inner awareness of being safe in your body. If you inadvertently disassociate or find fear taking over, stop moving and breathe deeply while re-connecting to your boundaries. Above all, do not judge yourself. This is your dance and there are no wrong movements. You are in charge of the quantity and the quality of your movements. Know and feel that you are in control.

Continue working with different emotional states giving them physical expression while maintaining a sense of safety within. Own each movement and make it uniquely yours. No one can take away your feelings or choice of expression. You are free to exhibit who you are right now in this body. Notice if your movement patterns are continuous or if you have flows of movements and periods of rest. Establish your own repetitive style or continue choosing to dance with diversity.

You may take ten minutes for this section or longer. Definitely take as long as you need to establish safety while moving and displaying different emotions kinesthetically. You may, of course, work with only one emotion for the entire session. Do what comes easily. Do not strain or force any issues that you feel uncomfortable with. This is your time to establish comfort within yourself according to your timetable and not someone else's.

As you complete this section close your eyes again and take a few moments to just feel your entire body. Be aware of your body's temperature, energy flow, and any other sensations. Bask for a moment in being physically you, just as you are. As you open your eyes gently scan your boundaries again and then take some time to write about your images, feelings, and thoughts. You may want to share the process with a close friend, or your therapist, or keep the journal just for yourself.

Points to Remember

As you repeat the exercises in this section, you are also building skills. It is as important for you to allow full expression of the emotions that caused you to feel unsafe or uncomfortable in your body, as it is to inaugurate new feelings and boundaries that insure your sense of feeling at home again. The expression of the old traumatic memories on a kinesthetic level allows them to "step out" into the open where they can be consciously released. Then, reclaiming appropriate boundaries and safety is more easily attainable. As you dance, you are also rekindling a sense of value and self-worth in the body. It is an affirmation of reclaiming your own body and the right to feel safe and at home.

Section II: Turning Lead into Gold

Musical Selections: *"Bell Born"* by Michael Mantra. Look for it in your local bookstore, or it may be ordered directly by writing Tranquil Technology Music, P.O. Box 20463, Oakland, Ca. 94620. If you cannot obtain *"Bell Born"* substitute *"Passion"* by Peter Gabriel or use any music without lyrics that has a variety of tones and sounds including those that are dissonant. We will also be moving in this section for about twenty minutes.

Read over this section and then record the paragraphs that seem most pertinent to you. If you are doing both sections in one session, skip the Breathing, Boundaries, and Inventory and go directly to the instructions following the inventory. If you are doing this exercise section separately, start here.

Breathing

Find a spot in the room that you feel comfortable in and have the physical dimensions to move in all directions without bumping into anything. Lie down on your back with your feet straight in front of you and your arms comfortably by your side. Close your eyes.

Begin now by taking some deep *complete breaths* the way you were instructed in Chapter Two for at least five rounds and then allow the natural rhythm of your breath to return. Just observe the natural rhythm of your breath for another five rounds. Allow this natural flow of the in breath and the out breath to be the gage for the rhythm in your movement patterns.

Boundaries

Become aware of your physical boundaries. You will define your physical boundaries through the skin on the surface of your body, which differentiates you from the floor, the air, the music, and even the instructions in this section. Touch your skin with your hands so that you know where your body's surface begins and ends. Make sure there's no place on your skin that is numb or undefined where you can disassociate from your body. Take as long as you need to identify your outer boundaries thoroughly. (Pause)

Once you have defined your physical boundaries, mentally go inside your skin and make the space on the inside as spacious and secure as you can conceive. There should be no feeling of restriction here. These are your inner boundaries. It is on the inside that you can safely house your memories, feelings, images and inner child.

Physical, Mental, Emotional, and Spiritual Inventory

Now be aware of your physical body. Notice any heat or cold, comfort or discomfort. Be aware of your energy level. Do you feel tired or invigorated? Do not feel like you have to change anything. Just observe your physical body without judgment for thirty seconds to a minute. Change your focus to your mental state. Is your mind quiet or full of chatter? What is the quality of your thoughts? Simply observe your mental state for about thirty seconds. Now check in with your emotional state. What feelings are available to you right now? Sadness?

Joy? Anger? Numbness? Neutrality? Without judging just notice what you feel. Last but not least become aware of the witness. It is the part of you that no matter what you have gone through is always OK. It is the knower in you who remembers your dreams. You may also call this part source, spirit, or soul. Locate the witness somewhere in your physical body. You may find it in your heart, solar plexus, or anywhere else.

After you have warmed up with the Movement Vocabulary in Chapter Two and feel ready to proceed, close your eyes again. Think of something that no longer works for you in your adult life. Perhaps it is a behavior or response that you learned as a child or even something that you developed out of the need to survive your childhood. It may be something that may have come out of your pain and wounding. Like Byron, as a child you may have learned that expressing your feelings equated pain and ridicule so you shut them down and as an adult that denial prevents you from experiencing joy and pain as well as the possibility of an intimate relationship.

If you were sexually abused, you may have learned to disassociate from your body so that you could physically and emotionally survive the violation. As an adult you may find yourself constantly "spacing out" or unable to stay present in your physical body. It may also cause you to flit from one project to another never staying with something long enough to finish it successfully.

As a child you may have learned to shut down your ability to receive and instead sought out isolation. This allowed you to survive emotionally, but as an adult you are acutely aware of your loneliness and the emotional walls that keep you separate and limited in your capacity to receive or give to others.

Or you may have been sick a lot as a child and felt left out and different than your peers. If there is nothing from your childhood that you can recall, think of something that does not work for you today. It may be the way you react emotionally, something in your lifestyle, or the direction that your life is going. Find something that pertains to you.

Once you have chosen that quality or behavior that helped you to survive as a child, or worked for you previously as an adult, but is in some way no longer appropriate for you now, allow this part of you to come to mind. Begin to remember kinesthetically and to feel the pain that caused you to survive or act in this way. Let the body exhibit the feelings and the choice. Denying nothing let it be a dance of pride and survival, but also be aware of the hurt, the anger or any other dominant emotion. Let it all be moved. Continue for about ten minutes.

Now see how this quality or behavior might be translated into something positive and more supportive to both your inner child and adult. First feel that you are no longer in danger. Reclaim your boundaries and work with your breath until you know that you are presently safe in your body if that is an issue. If you learned to shut down your feelings, imagine yourself creatively and safely expressing your feelings without fear of retribution. If you learned to split from your body or flit, imagine yourself grounded and focused. Your feelings of isolation may be translated into independence and then interdependence. If you had been sick a lot, see yourself healthy and vibrant. Find your own image for transformation.

If you feel stuck, write about it for a few minutes. Then focus back on your body and begin to dance these new qualities and behavioral patterns. How does it feel to be grounded in your body and to move directly and in a focused manner? Let yourself dance different feelings. Experience the freedom of moving from one emotion to another. Feel connected as you move, powerful, alone and yet willing to connect to the floor, the air and others. Feel the shifts emotionally in your body. Don't worry about what your movements mean. Allow the body to lead you energetically.

Feel yourself fully integrated as you weave these new qualities from the old patterns. As you ground these movements in your body know that the possibility for re-direction is occurring right now. The movements made in this room are extending to the changes you can make in your daily life. Take from ten to fifteen minutes for this section.

Bring a closure to your movements by gradually bringing the body to a stillness. Observe your breath, your energy flow, and any sensations in the body. Take another moment to ground your feet to the floor and to mentally reframe your boundaries. As you open your eyes, take out your journal and write down your feelings, sensations, and comments about your physical process, and any other revelations that occurred to you during this session.

Points to Remember

Remember that you may move with your eyes closed or open, but keep your attention turned inward. You may repeat this session as often as you like. You can continue to work on the same issue or choose different patterns to work on each time. Every time you work with the body in this way, you are practicing this new awareness physically. Expect changes in your daily life, but remember to also honor yourself where you are. If you were able to get in touch with the past, understand that your inner child's painful pattern allowed you to survive. Graciously now, you can move beyond the limitations of the past to a greater wholeness.

Chapter Six:
Dance as Physical Healing

"There is no such thing as a wrong body for dance.
The wrong body is a sick body, and that can be corrected spiritually."
— *Marie Brooks*

Experiencing Physical Trauma

This chapter begins with an accident. Less than a mile from home, I was involved in a head-on automobile collision, and then taken by ambulance to the emergency room.

The policewoman at the scene told me I was a "sitting duck." According to the police report, the man who hit me was speeding at 60 mph in a 25 mph zone. Before he ran the red light where I was turning left, he cut off a number of cars and weaved in and out of the two-lane residential street. Although, I was initially relieved that I had not done anything to cause the accident, I felt equally uneasy at being labeled a victim.

Pain in my neck, back, and arms intensified in the hours following the crash. A doctor confirmed that I had sustained soft tissue damage, fractured ribs, and had also bruised my liver, gall bladder and possibly other organs. Later that week I developed gastro-intestinal problems that did not respond to conventional treatment and remained undiagnosed for over five months. I also experienced constant headaches. I began to feel angry, out of control, and very much like a victim. What I wanted to do was forget the whole thing and go forward with my life. But the pain, headaches and other physiological responses over which I seemed to have no control, demanded otherwise.

About a week and a half after the accident, I woke up in the middle of the night for no apparent reason and shot straight up in bed as if someone had entered the room. My heart was pounding and I was in a sheer state of panic. The following day I was brought to this level of fear several times again by random noises or interruptions. Because of my experience with clients diagnosed with Post Traumatic Stress Disorder, I concluded that the fear had frozen in my body and that the trauma of the accident had triggered emotionally charged but unrelated memories from the past.

During the day, the fear seemed to be activated by noises or abrupt movements then extended to a sleep disorder that I had never experienced before and seemed to have no control over. Just as I would start to drift into sleep, I would be awakened with a jolt. It felt like I was being jerked back into my body and I experienced a rush of fear in the area of my heart. This sometimes happened as many as thirty times in one night.

I had to learn why this accident was causing me so much trauma. What was my body trying to tell me? I realized that the physical trauma had apparently triggered an emotional counterpart, and that in order to heal I had to deal with both. First I had to confront, express, and then release my anger, and then I had to deal with my fears even though they seemed irrational and unrelated to my present circumstances. I also needed to rebuild the relationship with my body.

One month after the accident I was still suffering from headaches and constant pain in my stomach. My body was as stiff as a board and I had to lead a workshop. The themes of the workshop included exploring the *sacred and the feelings of empowerment* in the body. My own body felt anything but sacred or empowered!

Conducting the workshop was a profound personal learning experience. Half way through the session, I realized that I had divorced myself from my own body. I felt completely alienated from my organs and at war with parts of my body. It seemed so automatic to want to resist the pain, and the longer my symptoms remained undiagnosed, the stronger the sensation of feeling out of control and victimized. My stomach was this "thing" that was causing me pain. All I wanted to do was take a pill and be rid of the discomfort.

It was in the workshop that I realized how distant I had become from myself. My stomach seemed to be the seat of pain, but it was certainly not a "thing" that I could cast out. As I softened around the pain, I knew that my healing was dependent on my relationship with my body, and that up to this point, all I had been doing was building internal walls.

Out of this realization, I made a shift that allowed me to approach my healing in a very different manner. I was able to acknowledge my feelings including anger. I stopped fighting myself, and that eased the sensation of feeling so out of control. I also stopped looking to others for all the answers and began to again trust my own body's innate wisdom.

Until I made this internal shift, I had felt like a disassembled jigsaw puzzle. Being referred to an internist, an orthopedic surgeon, a gastro endocrinologist, a radiologist, a chiropractor, a massage therapist, a physical therapist, and a trauma counselor only emphasized my sense of fragmentation. Everyone was a specialist. Sometimes I felt like leaving myself at home and just taking the specific body parts to each practitioner.

Most of the doctors and specialists were occupied with diagnosing my symptoms and trying to find suitable medication instead of engaging me in the healing process. They all acknowledged that the stress and trauma of the accident were contributing to my medical problems, but they did not offer solutions or pathways that could lead me to a creative resolution. Yet I had learned that my body's symptoms were inextricably linked to my emotions and spirit and that my mental frame of mind was both a trigger point and a controlling factor. The bottom line was trust and integration. My body was the site of the trauma and pain, but it also, I believed, held the correct solutions for healing. It was not unlike working with survivors of childhood abuse where the body symptomatically revealed the emotional trauma. At first I classified the accident as different since the cause was purely "physical." The accident showed me that physical cannot be separated from mental, emotional, and spiritual.

I also recognized that the body does not have "time lines." It can bring seemingly unrelated memories or emotions from the past into the present and future. My goal was to re-establish balance and health. This demanded that I embrace, rather then reject, all that stood in the way of my goal including the pain itself.

The complexity of diagnosing my internal injuries and the corresponding strong emotional responses made me aware of the energy and emotional shifts that had corresponding physical reactions. Up until the accident, I knew that physical symptoms including pain and illness were often the body's way of communicating feelings, stress, and sometimes unresolved issues. I had learned to respect the intricate way that the body recorded all of our thoughts and impulses and to use Movement for the Mind as a vehicle to express and unravel the body's messages. But because I had never experienced chronic pain or severe physical limitations, I had no direct knowledge of treating these symptoms in the same way. As long as I treated the effects of the accident as an outside occurrence and the subsequent pain as separate from myself, I remained angry, frustrated, and very much powerless over it's limiting hold on me, nor did my symptoms improve. When I was finally able to embrace the accident, the pain, and the fears as a part of myself, my body began to heal and the pain and fears also subsided. It was as if an internal wall of resistance just dissolved.

At the same time that I was struggling with my own healing, individuals in my classes and workshops started to come forward with stories of living with chronic pain and physical problems. I was shocked to discover just how many people lived with some kind of a physical disorder. All had sought medical help and were still coping with their problems.

The Body/Mind Connection and Healing

As much as our medical technologies are growing more sophisticated, and medical experts are providing better and better descriptions of how our bodies function, these advances often lead us to view the body as a kind of intricate machine. Such a view encourages us to see ourselves as a collection of fragments — a far cry from the integrated being we are whose body, mind, psyche, and spirit can be all focused on the task of healing.

Noted medical authors Bernie Siegel, Norman Cousins, Leonard Laslow, Deepak Chopra, and Andrew Weil are among an emerging group of physicians who are offering a holistic model in treating their patients. They are recognizing that a patient's attitude and participation are as essential to successful treatment as the medications they prescribe. Most significantly these doctors are affirming that health and well-being are part of a dynamic relationship that the individual maintains within him or herself. This dynamic relationship when disturbed can create an imbalance that affects the whole system. Whether the upset is physical, emotional, mental, or spiritual the whole person experiences the disturbance.

Psychoneuroimmunology (PNI), a branch of science that I mentioned in Chapters One and Three, is studying this link between emotions and the body and its affect on the immune system. Researchers in PNI have discovered that nerve cells directly connect to the immune system, and that chemicals produced by the brain can alter our physical body. The neuropeptides that can both cause and alleviate stress-related symptoms in the body also can affect our potential for healing. What we think, feel, and do has a direct relationship to our present and future health.

But what kind of health should we be seeking? What is "healing"? Just as the conventional medical model often fails to recognize the need to engage the mind, emotions, and spirit in treatment, we must not forget that healing from a physical ailment often also requires the embrace of the mind, psyche, and spirit.

Healing can come in many forms. For some it will mean the immediate reversal of a disease. For others, it will involve a shift in attitude followed by physical changes. There are also individuals who do not experience a noticeable improvement in their physical condition or who die, but that does not mean that they do not experience a healing.

Sometimes the body offers a lesson that an individual would never have learned without the physical limitation. Adversity can bring great things. It can bring estranged families back together. It can foster forgiveness and summon the deepest levels of compassion and honesty. We may not heal the physical body, but the mind, emotions, and spirit are healed in the process.

At other times, pain and illness can cause an estrangement where we experience our own bodies as the enemy. When we are at war with ourselves, there is little room for healing. For example, a large part of my own distress after my accident stemmed from feeling out of control with my body. Learning to reconnect on the inside, stimulates the body's natural healing mechanisms and allows for a much more relaxed state of body and mind which then can be receptive to healing.

This chapter includes the stories of a number of people who sought movement as a last resort and as an activity unrelated to their physical pain, and then found that it offered a pathway back to trusting their bodies and to creating a relationship of working with, rather then fighting against, themselves. Movement for the Mind offered each of them a way to communicate and alter their body image. They were able to make a conscious connection between their emotions, mental state, and their physical bodies. As a result, many of them were able to release outdated or limiting beliefs that were undermining their physical well-being.

Movement for the Mind is a vehicle for greater understanding that can result in healing. Too often we ignore the intelligence and wisdom that lies within each of us. Instead of just relying on external opinions, our bodies can also speak to us in their own language and reveal the information we need. Movement for the Mind helps us to understand the body's intelligence and to directly experience the integrative process. Using Movement for the Mind for healing connects us back to ourselves and helps to unveil our mysteries. It gives us a first hand experience of the body/mind connection. By experiencing the mental insights and emotional states while moving, physical changes occur naturally and spontaneously. These are the very results that scientists are so eagerly studying. Although Movement for the Mind, like other alternative therapies, is not necessarily a substitute for medication or surgery, it does offer a vital tool.

There are three stages to using Movement for the Mind for healing. First, participants are encouraged to acknowledge and express their feelings, especially if they feel victimized or feel like they have no control over their bodies. While it is never "wrong" to have feelings, both holding onto and repressing them can create problems. Expressing emotions allows an individual to unfold the next step in his or her healing process.

Second, through movement and imagery, participants ask questions about their illnesses and listen for the answer, thereby re-establishing a dialogue with themselves. This is a lesson in trusting the body's innate wisdom and intelligence. Participants may recall memories or feel emotions from the past that are seemingly unrelated to their illness. This is a signal to look at what may be unfinished business, and to finish it.

Third, participants are encouraged to become active in their healing processes by embracing their fears and pain as part of themselves. This allows them to release what is not in their control, and to feel safety in what is.

Movement for the Mind, through its inclusion of the body and emphasis on expression, awareness, and integration, can provide a vital tool for healing and an adjunct to modern medicine.

Shirley's Story

Shirley suffered from chronic arthritis. She was in her late thirties and moderately overweight. She had enrolled in one of my yoga classes and decided to take a workshop series. Within weeks she noticed a change in her body. The yoga classes gave her an increased range of motion. The arthritis had not disappeared but her stiffness had significantly been reduced.

The movement workshops allowed her to learn more about herself and her relationship with her body. In one workshop she discovered that as a little girl her body image had been stiff and awkward. She shared, "When I played with the other children on the playground I always felt uncoordinated and left out. On teams I would be the last one chosen, so I just stopped playing with them."

Her movement vocabulary that reflected her past was bound and controlled. Shirley realized that "stiffness" had been a way to shut out the actions of others and the subsequent pain of feeling left out and different. Her bound movements created a wall that others could not penetrate. She learned how to feel safe inside this "concrete" wall.

In one workshop she experimented with loose flowing movements and entertained a freedom that she had not felt in years. She was surprised at how good she felt. Although the arthritis did not disappear overnight, she realized that moving stiffly was part of a movement pattern that she established as a child. For Shirley this body awareness opened her to parts of herself that she had shut down. She too, had separated herself from her body and accepted the arthritis as a condition over which she had no control or connection.

Shirley's goal, which she fully explored in the Movement for the Mind sessions, was to reconnect to her body and to create new choices for moving in her life. Shirley made a conscious decision to treat and see her body in a new light. For her, it was the halfway point to healing her arthritis and to moving more freely in spite of it.

Karen's Story

Karen, a woman in her early forties, came to two Movement for the Mind workshops and then saw me for a private session. She had been attracted to the workshop flyer because she loved to dance. She in no way associated that the workshop could help her with what she felt was purely a medical problem.

Karen complained of a chronic pain along the lower left side of her body. She'd been to dozens of medical doctors and specialists. After a battery of tests revealed nothing, one doctor concluded that the pain might be related to prior back surgery. She continued to seek counsel from others. She went to several chiropractors, tried special cleansing diets, and ultimately felt more confused and out of control then ever.

In the private session, Karen told me that she also had been seeing a psychiatrist for depression. In the last two years she finalized a divorce after seventeen years of marriage, and had gotten addicted to tranquilizers. When we began to explore the pain through movement, her body froze and she became extremely frightened and ended the session.

Karen admitted, "I am afraid of letting my feelings out because I don't want to deal with what I might find out. I don't want more pain in my life." She felt comfortable seeing the psychiatrist because she could talk about various events, her emotions, and still avoid feeling them. She was very conscious of a lurking but forgotten memory that held so much fear for her that she did whatever she could to avoid facing it. She then stated that depression first began to haunt her when she was twenty years old.

It had never occurred to her or to any of the numerous medical advisers that her pain, the stresses in her life, and her fears might be connected. Everyone was trying to find outside ways to fix her. They prescribed surgery, drugs, diets, and physical manipulations, but none of these approaches encouraged her to connect with her own body or to strengthen the knowledge within herself. It was clear that when Karen came to see me she was divorced not only from her husband, but also from herself and that she had given others almost total control over her body and the power to take away her pain. I, too, understood this desperation.

Karen came to a few more private sessions, but chose not to explore the feelings she was working so hard to avoid. Every time I had her simply explore her physical sensations and move with the pain on her left side, she would hit an emotional wall that caused her to stop. While Karen wanted desperately to figure out what was causing her so much physical pain, she refused to look at what was creating her emotional trauma. Because of her dread of dealing with these emotions, whether or not the physical pain and emotional trauma were related, became insignificant and unexplored. Karen's experience with Movement for the Mind took her to this bridge of insight, but it was up to her to choose whether she wanted to cross it.

Angelica's Story:
Interrupting the Role of Victim

So often when pain or sickness become chronic or life threatening, we feel out of control. Not only can we begin to feel victimized by the circumstances that caused the changes in our physical body, but we also sometimes take on the role of victim. By succumbing to this role we actually impede the healing process. Playing victim robs us of hope, participation, integrity, and choice. If healing is about transformation, being a victim is about staying stuck. Over time, for some this role becomes a way of life, and the first step to wellness is to change that role identification. Angelica made such a change.

Angelica was twenty-four years old and her chronic pain had been diagnosed as Fibromyalgia. Angelica had been to dozens of doctors and specialists. She was also taking various medications. She was referred to me by her chiropractor as a last resort because nothing else seemed to be working.

Her pain was so severe at times that she would crawl into bed, hold her head, and sob for hours. She felt like a social outcast because no one seemed to understand why she was always suffering. She was tall, thin, attractive, and very creative. "How could a young person have so much pain?" She shouted one day. "Everyone asks me this." Even her doctors seemed impatient with her complaints and had no idea how to help her.

As a child she had hoped to become a professional ice skater, and had also studied modern dance and ballet before the Fibromyalgia forced her to stop at the age of thirteen. When we began to explore her past through Movement for the Mind, two strong themes emerged. One theme was that she had merged her own identity with that of her mother's. The second revealed that her mother was always sick, and felt helpless and at the constant effect of outer circumstances.

Angelica had been separated from her father at an early age and became her mother's confidante and best friend. Her mother, who meant well, was more like a child herself and leaned on Angelica for support and companionship. In the Movement for the Mind sessions, Angelica discovered that rather then abandoning her mother and becoming independent, she became just like her. She, like her mother, had taken on the role of a victim in every area of her life, and her relationship with her body was the central focal point.

No matter how negative or painful a pattern may be, it does serve some need or it would never have become a habit in the first place. Angelica finally realized this, and was so fed up with her discomfort and lifestyle that she was willing to examine all the ways that her pain and the role of victim fulfilled her. She discovered, "I became just like my mother who I wanted to feel close to. Pain got me out of situations that were uncomfortable or that I didn't want to deal with. I guess I also received attention and sympathy, and I knew how to play the role of someone who was always having something go wrong. Living like this, as awful as it is, has become comfortable." She admitted that her disease had become the center of her life.

It takes a lot of courage to examine what part we play in everything that occurs in our life. To take this kind of responsibility, of how we respond to things internally, allows us the freedom to shift things externally.

The Movement for the Mind sessions for Angelica were a balanced blend between physical movement and mental discipline. We worked as hard at releasing negative patterns of thought as we did at reconditioning her body to be a vehicle for joy and gentle kindness. When we started the sessions she was her own worse critic and had no clue about how to treat her body with respect, consideration, or moderation. In her daily activities, she either pushed herself until she collapsed or she would flake out of her responsibilities when the pain got too much for her to bear.

Originally, I had intended to work with movements that could increase mobility and relieve some of the stiffness that she also suffered from. But as her story unfolded it became apparent that Angelica's mental and emotional states were inextricably tied to her physical condition, and I trusted that the pain would diminish as the other issues were cleared and re-directed. The majority of the sessions held a three-pronged format. Each session unraveled the strong hold that the role of victim had on her. Then we would shift the feelings in her body, and create a new vocabulary that replaced strength and power in all the places that she felt victimized and out of control. Instead of feeling enmeshed with her mother, she created boundaries reclaiming her own unique identity. She was able to retain a close relationship with her mother without making her wrong, and developed compassion both for herself and for her mother.

Physically things began to change for Angelica. She learned how to respect her body and her specific needs. She had more good days then bad days. The headaches that used to incapacitate her were less severe and less frequent. Her friends, boyfriend, and even her mother noticed the changes in her. She shared during one of our last sessions, "I'm actually happy for maybe the first time in my life. I'm learning to let go of pain in every area of my life. Things are going well."

Role of Body Image in Healing

When the psyche detaches itself from or is at odds with the body, it affects our receptivity to heal and our capacity to maintain wellness. Bringing back dignity in the body when there has been a great deal of physical pain, loss, or long periods of sickness is as essential to healing as the physical miracles we accomplish with medication and surgery. Sustaining a healthy body image reflects the integration between body and mind and is a necessary component to experiencing wholeness.

Some forms of illness leave a permanent scar that goes deeper than the skin. For example, working with several groups of women diagnosed with breast cancer, a major theme that emerged from our work was the role of body image. These women were all in support groups designed to help them deal with their feelings of the trauma of surgery, radiation, and chemotherapy. Most of the women felt that the cancer had also robbed them of their image of themselves. Some women felt this overtly and some more subtly. Although we could discuss this, none of them felt any resolution until we began to work with Movement for the Mind sessions.

In one movement workshop after the warm up, I had the group explore their feelings about themselves and their lives before they were diagnosed with cancer. Each woman moved using physical movement and mental images. After about ten minutes, I asked them to bring to mind images of themselves and their reactions when they were first diagnosed with cancer. I encouraged the women to give themselves one hundred per cent permission to explore, through the use of movement, the full range of their feelings. Their limbs echoed the language of their hearts, hopes, and fears.

I asked them to dance each stage of feeling and reaction. Shock, denial, anger, grief, fear, and despair got a chance to be expressed and also to be released. Then I invited them to give the cancer permission to talk through their bodies. The cancer symbolically took on a form that revealed its intention and message. Instead of merely viewing the cancer as this foreign thing outside that had invaded them, they had an opportunity to dialogue with the cancer.

Every part of them got a chance to express itself. Because the session brought up strong emotions, we took some time after this session to debrief verbally and to write in journals for about fifteen minutes. Then we began moving again. I brought them back to present time and had them explore their bodies, as they perceived them today. I had them fully embody what was missing, what made them feel less vital, less like a person, and any other sensation.

Finally, I asked them to bring back the pre-diagnosis images they had danced with, and had them include the messages that the cancer had revealed so that they could create a new experience of themselves and their bodies. This new experience was to include the lessons they had learned, the courage and strength of their trials, and the totality of themselves. The women who existed before the cancer was not to be left behind, but had to be brought into the present. I asked them to create an image of themselves that represented renewal and the future. We created closure with this dance and then came together in a circle for debriefing.

Each segment was not only revealing but also cathartic in ways none of the women expected. Perhaps the most significant and surprising section was the part where each woman dialogued with her cancer. One woman shared, "When you asked us to bring in the cancer and let it talk and express, I thought no way. I'm not letting this thing that has almost destroyed my life any more attention or energy. But when I did, I couldn't believe what it said. I got in touch with anger, sadness, and this horrible critical part of me. Just to see this took a load off of me. It made me aware of how hard I am on myself, how much I hold inside, and how I've got to let go of the resentment and judgment that I've kept stuffed inside of me for so long. I feel freer right now than I ever have before."

The most profound realization for most of the women was how alienated they felt from themselves and their bodies. The cancer had caused not just a physical rift but also one that extended to their psyche and that affected everything else. Rebuilding a body image that both reflected who they've always been in spite of the cancer and who they had become as a result of this experience was essential.

One woman spoke for many others in the group; as we listened heads nodded in agreement. "I've had a really hard time. Who I thought I was seemed to disappear with the cancer. My looks, my social life, the focus of my life, and what I thought were important all got challenged. Now that I'm in remission, my values have changed and that is good, but I also lost a big part. The cancer caused me to mistrust my body. Before this session I had been walking around kind of numb, like I wasn't really in this body. Now I realize I've got to take a stand, literally, for who I've become. Everything has changed and nothing has changed. I forgot that. I actually feel like me again. It's OK to be in my skin; in fact it feels pretty darn terrific!"

Sheila's Story: Experiencing the Body Free of Pain — a Body/Mind Healing

Sheila was in her early fifties, the wife of a physician, and had been suffering from Fibromyalgia for about seven years. She had been to the best doctors and was on several medications to help her sleep and to keep her pain tolerable. No doctors seemed to be able to reverse her condition, and even her husband felt helpless in his efforts to get her help.

She, like so many, was a closet dancer. "I've always loved to dance," she confided to me, "but I've been in so much pain physically that I've barely been able to walk." She was a woman who was always trying to please others and who often took on more than her share of responsibility. She reluctantly admitted that her "crime" was probably trying to be the best wife, mother, and family social director.

It seemed to me after our initial consultation that the missing ingredient in Sheila's life was joy. Her daily activities were burdened with duty and her body was racked with pain. I decided to spend our first session recreating the sensation of joy in her body. For the entire hour she explored feelings that she had forgotten existed. "Freedom, terrific, fun, happiness, sunshine, laughter, lightness, playfulness, silliness, and wonder" were the words that she translated into physical movement. She had a smile on her face the entire session and her body reflected this vibrancy as she sat down after her dance. She shared little about her experience except to say that she felt terrific and loved the dancing and the whole process. She made another appointment to see me and then left my office.

One week later I received a phone call from Sheila. Her voice had a newfound lilt to it. She told me "I feel like a new person. I have been pain free since our session. I feel so good that I don't need any more sessions, but I'd like to take any movement class that you offer in the future. I've got to include dance as part of my life." After a few more minutes of conversation, she thanked me profusely and asked me to keep her on my mailing list.

Sheila moved about two months after her phone call to me and I lost track of her, so I do not know if she was able to sustain her "miraculous" recovery. I do know that through Movement for the Mind, she tapped into something both mysterious and extraordinary. It is the stuff that in the West, we might call a Peak Experience and in the East, Zen Masters would call Satori. Scientifically, one could hypothesize that Sheila's active state of joy acted on her own brain chemistry to release powerful neuropeptides, not unlike endorphins, that actually caused an emotional and physical shift in her body.

Movement for the Mind provided an integrated system for Sheila. She fully engaged her body, mind, and emotions in a perceptual reality that was juxtaposed to what had become the norm for her. Instead of experiencing pain, she was able to completely surrender to joy and to access a state of consciousness that translated itself into physical reality.

Exercise: Dance as Healing

The following exercise can be used to release pain, to better understand your illness, to improve your body image, and to help you to get in touch with any of the feelings that your physical condition has caused you.

As in each previous chapter, if you have the time, you'll want to first warm up with the Movement Vocabulary in Chapter Two. Once you are familiar with these principles you can go on to this section. Before you begin the session survey your room and make sure you have the privacy and space that you need without bumping into anything. Any room will do as long as you can stretch out and take several large steps in all directions. Take off your shoes, place them out of your way and then leave your voice of judgment with your shoes.

After you have completed the exercises, write down the feelings, memories or any other impulses that you may have experienced while moving. You may want to read what you have written out loud several times, but do not strain to intellectually figure out what happened. Allow the experience to remain as physical and emotional as you can, and trust that the insights needed will be revealed to you in an appropriate and timely manner. The most important point is to let your body do the communicating and to not judge or censor any of the movements or feelings. Again, remember to read the entire section through once and then you may want to record the instructions and move to the sound of your own voice pausing in the appropriate places to give yourself time to complete each task.

Musical Selections: Feel free to add music to your sessions. Remember that music is a motivator, it can support the environment that you are creating or it can work against it like a distraction. There will be three sections in this session. For the first section

I would like you to choose a piece of music that is pleasing and reflects your happiest self. *Timeless Motion* or Yanni's, *In my time,* are good selections. For the second section choose something dissonant and discordant. I often use Bell Born by Michael Mantra. For the last section, choose music that is upbeat and makes you feel triumphant and joyous. If you like music by Enya, that is a good choice, or you can select any piece that inspires you.

Breathing

Find a spot in the room that you feel comfortable in and have the physical dimensions to move in all directions without bumping into anything. Lie down on your back with your feet straight in front of you and your arms comfortably by your side. Close your eyes.

Begin now by taking some deep complete breaths the way you were instructed in Chapter Two for at least five rounds and then allow the natural rhythm of your breath to return. Just observe the natural rhythm of your breath for another five rounds. Allow this natural flow of the in breath and the out breath to be the gage for the rhythm in your movement patterns.

Boundaries

Become aware of your physical boundaries. You will define your physical boundaries through the skin on the surface of your body, which differentiates you from the floor, the air, the music and even the instructions in this section. Touch your skin with your hands so that you know where your body's surface begins and ends. Make sure there's no place on your skin that is numb or undefined where you can disassociate from your body. Take as long as you need to identify your outer boundaries thoroughly. (Pause)

Once you have defined your physical boundaries, mentally go inside your skin and make the space on the inside as spacious and secure as you can conceive. There should be no feelings of restriction here. These are your inner boundaries. It is on the inside that you can safely house your memories, feelings, dreams, images and inner child. No one can judge, change, or invalidate this place within your inner boundaries.

Physical, Mental, Emotional, and Spiritual Inventory

Now be aware of your physical body. Notice any heat or cold, comfort or discomfort. Be aware of your energy level. Do you feel tired or invigorated? Do not feel like you have to change anything. Just observe your physical body without judgment for thirty seconds to a minute. Change your focus to your mental state. Is your mind quiet or full of chatter? What is the quality of your thoughts? Simply observe your mental state for about thirty seconds. Now check in with your emotional state. What feelings are available to you right now? Sadness? Joy? Anger? Numbness? Neutrality? Without judging just notice what you feel. Last but not least become aware of what I call the witness. It is the part of you that no matter what you have gone through is always OK. It is the knower in you who remembers your dreams. You may also call this part source, spirit or soul. Locate the witness somewhere in your physical body. You may find it in your heart, solar plexus, or anywhere else.

Section I: Retrieving Yourself

After you have warmed up with the *Dance Principles* and feel ready to proceed, close your eyes again. You may be sitting, standing, or lying down. Picture yourself before you became ill or had to face the current physical condition that is causing you distress. It does not matter what this is. It could be a condition that occurred as a result of an accident similar to the one I experienced. You could be experiencing occasional headaches or dealing with a life threatening disease. It may even be the fear of aging and not having the energy and enthusiasm that you used to.

Allow yourself to fully engage your mind with these images. See yourself, how you look, what you're doing, how you feel, and any other details before this condition took place. Remember that you may feel these things rather than picture them. Incorporate your pictures or feelings into movement. Let your images fill your limbs and begin to move energetically as this earlier version of yourself. Feel the energy in your body, notice your emotions, and how you're moving. Is it fast or slow? Are you lying on the floor or jumping around the room? Is your mood peaceful, joyous, angry, depressed, or bursting with enthusiasm? Are you gregarious or needing solace and quiet? Remember don't judge what's going on, simply observe and keep moving with this past image of you for about five minutes.

Section II: Dialoguing with your Body and your Illness

Bring your movements to a closure but stay aware of how you feel in your body. Now bring to mind your fears, pain, or physical circumstances that you are currently dealing with. Let this physical condition take over. Imagine that your body is a theatrical stage. Allow the condition to move in its entirety over the stage of your body. Notice how it moves. Is it big or small, subtle or blatant, light or heavy? Where is it located? Does it take over your body or is it just in parts? Where is the center of your discomfort?

After you have moved letting the condition reveal itself in your body for about five minutes, begin to dialogue with it. Still moving, formulate questions you would like answers to. You may want to ask, what is your purpose? What do you need? Why do you need so much attention? Is there something you're trying to tell me? Then just be open. Notice your reactions. Follow whatever impulses occur to you spontaneously. Your movements may change. You may feel an influx of energy or you may suddenly feel frustrated. Observe all of it and keep on mentally dialoguing, moving, and listening through the mind and body for another five minutes. You may hear messages, or visualize images, or you may simply feel sensations.

If you have never done this exercise before you might be thinking, "Who am I dialoguing with anyway?" For centuries we have been told to trust others including professionals who may know very little about us. This process has the potential for allowing you to access the answers that lie within you. You and your body know more about what is going on inside of you than anyone else.

Section III: Integration

Again, let your movements come to a closure and mentally thank your pain or condition for sharing information, and then simultaneously visualize the condition outside of your body. Release it from every joint, muscle, tissue, cell, and molecule. Bring back the earlier images of yourself before you got sick and observe what part of you is presently missing. Were you happier then or were you depressed? Does this have anything to do with your current condition? Allow yourself to rekindle the positive attributes and to change the ones that no longer serve you.

Begin to create a dance out of these realizations. Combine the information that you just received with any observations that would contribute to a happier and healthier you. Let this dance change your body image to one that feels good to you. Feel the energy from the top of your head to the bottom of your feet. Engage every part of you in this expression. The most important part of this section is to participate fully. Claim your insights, observations, and feelings. Let your body do the talking. Even if there is little concrete mental information, sense the freedom in your body. Go with that and continue exploring and moving for another five to ten minutes.

Closure

Bring your movements to a closure by gently closing your eyes and by becoming aware of the natural rhythm of your breath, but this time retain your experience. Let each cell of your body reverberate with the present energy that you sense in your body. Feel it take permanent residence. You may lie back down on the floor, sit, or remain standing.

We will now repeat the inventory that we did at the beginning of the session. Be aware of your physical body. Notice if you feel differently than when you started. How? What are the sensations in your body? Is the pain or discomfort gone? (Pause) Now check in with your mental state. Is your mind quiet? What are the qualities of your thoughts? How is your mental state different then earlier? (Pause) Move on to your emotional state. Observe the colors in your emotional palette. Are there more feelings available to you now? What are they? (Pause) Then once again identify with the witness. Locate it physically and feel the part of you that is connected to spirit and to your source of knowledge. Take a couple of minutes to do this inventory mentally without judgment, and then return to observing your breath for a few more minutes.

Journaling

Feeling fully grounded in your body, with your boundaries intact, gently sit up and get your journal and pen. Begin to write. Let your hand flow like in previous journaling sections without censoring anything. Write your impressions, your insights, how you feel emotionally, what your dance meant, and how your body feels. Talk about your body image, the dialogue between your physical condition and yourself, and what changes you made in the final section. Just write. Don't worry about grammar or repetition. Do not strain. You may write for as long as you'd like.

You may have a lot to say or you may end up writing just a few sentences. Most importantly, stay connected to the feelings and sensations in your physical body and trust your insights.

Points to Remember

This session can be repeated as often as you like. If you are experiencing pain like Sheila or Angelica you may wish to first explore only slow, gentle movements. Gently see if you can invite a sensation other than pain. Be open to trusting your body again.

The purpose of the exercises in this chapter is to help you:

- Acknowledge and express your feelings. This releases stagnant energy from your body and reveals your emotional state, which may be contributing to your illness. You then have the choice of creating emotional states that can support your healing.

- Learn to dialogue with your pain or disease. This is a lesson in how to listen and then trust your own body's innate wisdom and intelligence.

- Become aware of how you felt before you got sick. This may give you clues about your illness and if it is connected to seemingly unrelated traumas from the past.

- Become active in your healing process. This frees you from taking on the role of victim and allows you to be more available to solutions and to feeling more in control of your body.

Having said that, I also want to add that sometimes we get sick and can't find any emotional or mental connections. Sometimes the only solution is to restore an inner experience of peace. The exercises in Chapter Three can also be used as a tool for releasing stress and for bringing a sense of harmony and connectedness back to the body.

Chapter Seven:
Sharing the Process

"I spent long days and nights in the studio seeking that dance which might be the divine expression of the human spirit through the medium of the body's movement...."

— *Isadora Duncan*

For me the path of dance and moving mindfully is most powerfully expressed through the experience of others. Others, who each exemplify their unique journey and yet share a fundamental core — the need to express, to love, to heal, to share themselves, to be free to laugh, to cry, to sing, to dance, and to create. In their own words here are some of their experiences of this path of Movement for the Mind.

My introduction to Dance began at the age of seven when my mother enrolled me in ballet school. From the start, I fell in love with the aesthetics of the art form and the beauty and grace of the dancer. However, as my training continued, I became increasingly frustrated with my body's limitations in perfecting the exacting technique of ballet and in conforming to the ideals of a dancer's body. This growing frustration led me to give up ballet at age sixteen. In college, I dabbled in modern and jazz dance classes, where I discovered a greater freedom of movement beyond the strict rules of ballet. However, throughout this entire period of my dance training, my experience of dance was limited to technical instruction. None of my training up to this point had anything to do with movement originating from within.

In my first Movement for the Mind workshop, I learned to emphasize feelings, not technique: allowing emotions or sensations to generate movement. From this and later workshops and classes, I began to learn the profoundness, passion and joy of movement that had always been lacking in my technical dance training. However, the depth of my experience was still limited because I was out of touch with myself and my feelings in many ways.

One of the key turning points in my life occurred in the "Dance of the Inner Child" workshop. In this workshop, a profound memory surfaced which eventually led me into therapy and the beginnings of allowing myself to open up to feelings I had previously sheltered myself from. After about a year of therapy and several workshops later, I was amazed at the depth of my experience. The information that came up, the feelings that surfaced, and the doors that opened within myself were much deeper than anything I had felt or known before.

In some of the other Movement for the Mind workshops, the frequency of the sessions and the willingness of the participants to share very vulnerable parts of themselves, created an environment of safety and trust that allowed me to explore some very unknown and scary places, as well as places of great strength and joy. These workshops enhanced both my verbal skills and my ability to direct the shifts beginning to occur in my daily life. Ultimately, my experiences with dance, moving from this place of creativity, have been critical catalysts in my process of self-discovery and continually serve to open new doors in my search for understanding and wholeness.

— Diana

I did a Movement for the Mind session recently to clear some body issues I was having. Since I work in the field of counseling and spiritual guidance for others, I don't often feel the need to ask for help. However, I was experiencing a particularly difficult adjustment to a pending move out of state. I found that I was having a hard time staying in my body while I was trying to reconcile this decision and the ramifications of the move.

In doing the movement work with my body, I was suddenly aware of how much time I spend outside of it. I noticed that I don't often pay attention to anything below my neck. It is as if my body is this bubble that I visit. I operate on automatic pilot, and it is only when I am beset by a trauma that I'm suddenly aware of a body that feels out of control.

I was told to stand and feel my entire body and then to sit or lie down on the floor in whatever way was comfortable for me. Then I started to move to the conflicting voices inside my head. I found myself moving my arms and hands in an assault/ protective stance that webbed the entire span of my body. It was as if I was creating an invisible shield to protect the vulnerable parts of my body from attack. This surprised me! I never realized that I did anything to protect my body.

As I emptied everyone out of my head save for my own thoughts, the movements became graceful, and my hands and arms were inviting nourishment through their artful motions... again, all very surprising for someone who does little more in the realm of movement other than walk! I felt graciousness replace a sense of constriction, and soon I was releasing my feeling of being "split" between the needs and wants of others and the needs and wants of myself.

As I worked on this issue and moved back to a point of origin, all the time translating the intellectual understanding into a body action and reaction, images surfaced of myself as a little girl having to be very good so as not to disturb my father who was ill. I remembered that I could never show my exuberance because I was told it might overwhelm my father. One time when my mother was annoyed with my father for not feeling well, I told my mother we needed to be quieter for his sake. I was the child coming to the rescue of her parent! And how often I have played that role out again and again in this life.

As I looked at this, I thought about the price I had paid to protect and please others. As I cleared the insights through my body, I felt incredibly free and refreshed. By the time the session was over, I sensed that I was fully present in my body, and that I had come to an understanding about much of my dilemma that had not been obvious to me previously. I was truly amazed at the speed with which I was able to clear the "trauma" when I worked with my body as opposed to working from just a mental perspective. The body is so willing to engage and disengage from things that displace it, and I do not understand why we don't put much more emphasis on a full body approach to therapy and to living life.

In reviewing my experience with "dance," it seems that the body is always the final frontier or the final battleground in our concept of healing and well-being. In reality we should make it the first!

— Kathleen

The Movement for the Mind Sessions have offered me the space to go into a place I cannot enter by myself.

In the sessions, I have experienced that truth Isadora Duncan must have danced. It allows me to pour out a part of myself that has been longing for freedom and expression ever since I was a little girl of two.

— Natasha

Most days I am a very happy person. I am not wealthy but I have an abundance of everything I desire. I attribute my current happiness to the gift of cancer and the resulting transformation, which brought my body and mind back into balance. The numerous workshops I have participated in have played an important role in creating that balance.

Ever the skeptic, I was formally trained in mathematics and physics and spent the greater part of my adult life analyzing things. Engineers are trained to look for failure modes and design fault-tolerant systems. However, applying these skills to human relationship was a disaster for me. I was also an atheist and did not think of myself as a person that was self-reflective.

The Movement for the Mind sessions had an uncanny way of revealing my mental blind spots and bringing everything back into focus through my body. Through the course of this work I now know when I need to be reminded when I am off-center and in need of a spiritual body tune-up. Usually, the way it works for me is that the dance stops my mind from racing. My mind then becomes quiet and I get in touch with some very powerful visual imagery and insights.

In one workshop we were dancing to the elements: earth, water, air, and fire. I was not making any connection to earth or fire and felt like I was just going through the motions. But water and air for me were memorable. I began moving very slowly. I visualized a glacier, like the one that created the Yosemite Valley. I know that water always seeks its own level. The vessel, which holds it, determines its shape.

While moving, the element of water became a metaphor for the importance of surrender in my life. When I let go and give people and events the freedom to find their natural outcomes, like water, life flows smoothly. Yet from this place of surrender, like a glacier, I can carve a masterpiece much finer than anything I could have created from sheer willfulness. For me the words I had heard in a recent church sermon, "powerlessness is the turning point of real power" literally came alive for me. My dance reminded me that through surrender, I could have all the power of a glacier, adapt to any circumstance, and in the process turn my life into a work of art.

When I worked with the element air through movement, the image I formed was a hillside filled with redwoods shrouded in fog. My movements were rolling and lazy. There was natural beauty everywhere, and because I was light as air I could be everywhere at once and be totally immersed in the beauty of life.

This became a metaphor for the way I now understand God and my spirituality. I see it as a creative life force that animates every living being. The more I endeavored to connect with this life force, the more I could be surrounded by beauty. It takes a lot of work for me to find the beauty and goodness in the difficult people who come into my life and to move effortlessly in their midst. Yet my dance with the element air helped me to do just that.

The movement sessions also have allowed me to look at my dark side. In one session we were working in pairs and had the opportunity to look at relationship issues through movement. In a couple of hours I was able to see patterns that had occurred in my marriage and with a current relationship, but had never been able to acknowledge or change.

Because of that session, today I am able to look for the body language that signals the onset of those feelings of being pushed into a corner and trapped. I now try to bring it into my conscious awareness, and then engage my capacity to just back off and listen.

In another workshop, I remembered being ill at ease. I wasn't in the mood to dance or be mindful, but I had come to know that every time I did this work, there would be some new lesson, some new truth that would prove helpful to me. This workshop was no exception. In the movement session, my body was always going into balancing positions, not unlike the tree pose in yoga.

At first I thought this was just my yoga practice working its way into dance, but as I listened, my body was telling me that I needed greater balance in my life. I began to re-examine the things I was doing and saw that I was becoming too focused on the welfare of others and that I was neglecting my own welfare. After the session, I made a commitment to enjoying life more fully, to treating myself to fun activities, and to learning from my experience of recovering from cancer the importance of living life to its fullest, as if every day were my last.

To me these lessons became my "church" and these dance sessions had an uncanny way of bringing my spirituality to center stage through the body/mind connection.

— Patrick

The Movement for the Mind sessions have been an extremely healing process for me. When I look at myself now and compare myself to how I was before, I clearly see how much I have changed. Through experiencing this work I've been opened, touched, softened, and deepened. I feel more fully available to truly live my life in the present moment. I am joyfully alive and vibrant. Best of all, I feel more fully integrated.

I have always been a very "kinesthetic" type of person. It's easy for me to sense and feel when something is going on in my body (or more accurately my body/mind). Through the private sessions, I have been able to focus on these sensations, work with them, and process my emotions at a very deep level.

Each session usually begins with some debriefing. I share what has been going on for me. Verbally through discussion and questions, we find a focus for the session. Then through the process of relaxation, attention on my body senses, and my breath, I begin the experience of bringing to life aspects of myself that I have put aside and tried to ignore by focusing my energy through movement. Ironically, these ignored aspects are the ones still running my life. I use movement to bring these aspects into view, allowing me to fully feel all the feelings I had previously blocked. It always amazes me how quickly I am able to access old mindsets, belief systems, and perceptions. As I work with them re-experiencing my past realities, it becomes extremely validating for me. It also gives me choices and the capacity to change them.

For example, as a very young child I had an experience with my father that was both painful and confusing. Somehow I found a way to cope with that experience. At that time I didn't work through the pain and confusion; instead, I just found a coping mechanism to survive. Since my childhood was fairly chaotic, I got real practiced at coping. As a teenager I had another major experience that painfully impacted me concerning the same issue. Because I was a teenager and not a young child, I reacted differently to the same experience adding a new coping mechanism.

As an adult, I realized I had created a repertoire of dysfunctional coping mechanisms. None of the methods worked optimally, because they had been built out of fear and survival rather than through a healthy process of expressing my feelings and needs. Processing in these sessions has allowed me to shine a light on and to really feel and experience the stuck places in my body/mind. I experience that process as "dancing" my inner child or teenager (or whatever piece of me that is stuck). It is in the dancing that I have brought to life and fully experienced and embraced these ignored aspects of myself and integrated them. The Movement for the Mind sessions have taught me how to respect myself and to set boundaries and limits. As I become more aware and conscious of my body/mind, I become more integrated, whole, productive, and joyful in my life!

— Penelope

My livelihood as a computer analyst exercised my left brain, my masculine, analytical side. But I yearned for the balance to wake up my right brain, to activate my creative feminine side. Aikido (a Japanese martial art) stressed balance through symmetrical practice. Striving to accomplish symmetrical movements introduced me to the differences between the left and right sides of my body and how they worked. Next I wanted to move toward another kind of balance where I could integrate them.

I had participated in numerous drumming circles as a singer and drummer and became creatively comfortable sharing my stories, laughter and tears, and improvising songs and healing sounds. But I remained in awe (and sometimes aghast) of those who could also express themselves physically through movement. I had always felt awkward and inadequate dancing.

During regular massage and Reiki sessions, I began seeing images of colorful scenes and symbols. Through these images I discovered that my body acts as an antenna to provide new insights from a different perspective. For the first time in my life I wanted to paint and to move and dance!

I decided to take a Movement for the Mind workshop called "Spring into Action: a Body/Mind Workshop through Dance/Movement." The group was small, about twenty people, none of whom I knew (which helped). I quickly felt enthused, focused, excited, and safe in a friendly, free flowing professionally guided atmosphere. We started very slowly and basically (on the floor), so that I soon forgot my self-conscious inhibitions. With my eyes closed, I relaxed into the event. Surprisingly, it did not seem foreign to me. I had trained twenty years earlier in Aikido where a well executed movement felt and looked like musical, flowing energy. This time I created the movements myself. As time in the workshop progressed, I went deeper into myself and felt freer in my movements. My true self emerged, uninhibited, and in a strange but profound way uninhabited. I touched this deep unknown place inside of me.

I wanted to quiet my intellect and my constant need to analyze, and experience the workshop from my creative and higher self. As a result, I do not remember all the steps or progressions and how they came about. I just remember some of the feelings of inner joy and ecstasy that I got from getting in touch with myself. We were told to visualize what we wanted to feel, become, and work on. I danced that joy and created my imagery, and in the process they evolved together.

When I got home, I reproduced my dance as an 18x24 pastel drawing. Three years later, that image still evokes the memory of sensual joy at opening my creative center. I see new growth welling up from the luminous, voluptuous orbs dynamically grounded, yet reaching and growing towards a higher awareness. The palms of my hands still buzz when I study the picture, just as they did when I danced it. I realize even now that each new step in getting to know who I am and who I can become brings rewarding results.

Previously my art was generated from landscapes or photographs. This was the first time I was able to create a drawing from my mind. My dancing had unlocked the creative energy within me, and gave me the ability to express it on paper as a bonus! It personified all that I had felt in my body: vitality, aliveness, sensuality, softness and radiance. I called my pastel , "My spirit is one with being female."

— Judy

When I decided to try movement therapy and to engage in The Movement for the Mind sessions, I had been in Client Centered Therapy for several years. I was finding that, as good as this "talk" therapy was for coming to an understanding of my issues and feelings, I was having trouble getting in touch with what my feelings actually were. On more than one occasion I would be describing a painful event from my childhood in an ordinary conversational tone of voice, my therapist would stop me and ask me what I was feeling, and I would not be able to tell her. I had to learn how to pay attention to the sensations in my body and identify what they meant through verbal descriptions.

In the Movement for the Mind sessions, the process was much more direct. As the images I describe below illustrate, Movement for the Mind introduced me to a realm of clear and graphic landscapes saturated with emotional content. This direct access to extremely meaningful personal images focused my efforts in therapy bringing desired results, and opening a new dimension of creativity in my daily life. I have found that for me every creative act is in some way a self-portrait. Being able to explore my inner landscapes has allowed me to tap into a source of creativity that I had not known existed and to resolve issues that before had been merely talk. It has literally opened up a new world for me.

For example, as I listened to the guided imagery for grounding and changing my walk, my eyes closed as I stood there. I felt my feet fully contact the floor. I imagined that my *feet reached deeply to the center of the earth anchored by all that is rich, sturdy, and grounded. As I began to move these images flooded my mind and body:*

I am at the earth's core. This is my domain. Fire is the air I breathe. Magma flows in my veins. My work is sculpting this planet, lifting mountains, moving continents, closing oceans, opening rifts. Volcanoes are my laughter, earth-quakes are my smile. I am the living core of this planet. I am its life force.

Another time while moving and opening to the wounded places inside of me with the help of guided imagery to heal my inner child, these thoughts danced in my mind while my body reflected their images. I visualize myself with my wounded inner children. Protecting them, I let them know that they are safe. I am standing on a tall red mesa. Through the clear air I can see for hundreds of miles in all directions.

I am wrapped in a white blanket. On my head is a black hat with a feather stuck in the hatband. I am a shaman. With me are three children, myself at five, myself at ten, and myself at fifteen. They want to play and I give them permission. I bathe them in white light so that when they run   off the edge of the mesa, they soar instead of fall. Higher and higher they soar until they are only specks, but I always know where they are and I always know that they are safe. I am there with them. I am standing on the mesa and I am soaring in the air with my children at the same time. Eventually night starts to fall and the air turns cold. My children return to earth. I open my blanket and they walk straight into the center of my body. There I wrap them up warm for the night.

— Frank

Off and on over the years, I have worked with traditional psychotherapists, sitting and analyzing the issues in my life. Since my body was at the core of my issues, I decided I needed to include a physical approach as well as a psychological one to create balance in my life. When I started working with the Movement for the Mind approach in private sessions, it helped me connect the thoughts in my head with the emotions and feelings in my body. I didn't realize that it would also touch me deeply in my soul.

I looked forward to this time; time for myself. Time to practice opening up and sharing my feelings, something I was never encouraged to do as a child. I would come in and sit on the floor, stretching out as I began to relax. I knew that I was in the right place.

In one session while moving, I was verbally guided to visualize cutting away "tentacles" that represented old beliefs and judgments that no longer served me. The tentacles attached to my body related to my physical size. Looking back now, I can see that I was a tall girl at twelve, who was naturally gaining a few pounds as I went through puberty. The tentacles for me represented judgmental messages from others like: "There is something wrong with you. Why can't you lose weight? You shouldn't eat that. You would be so pretty if only you could lose weight."

The tentacles kept me tied down. Since I was twelve, these messages have dominated my life. I am tired of spending so much energy struggling with these issues. I want to be free of the tentacles. Part of me is scared of letting go of these familiar feelings, as though putting these ideas out of my head means that there is nothing to keep me in line. But another part of me feels so free when I visualize cutting away the tentacles. I am learning to trust myself and to substitute discipline for the beliefs and values enforced and imposed upon me from others.

I imagined standing free of these mental, emotional, and physical tentacles and just being in empty space. In the first instant, I felt a bit anxious and apprehensive with the concept of "emptiness," but very quickly I felt a sense of peace and strength in that empty space. While literally moving in this "space," I realized that my search for the answers to some of my questions had to begin right here.

In another session, I learned how to move in my body and express the feelings of the girl I was before I was twelve years old and received all of the negative messages that I now call my "tentacles." What joy and freedom I felt inside. My body moved easily and felt light, a sensation I have not felt in years. I remembered how it felt to run and play and just have fun.

Then I see myself as twelve again. My body feels heavier and slower. I remember how it is to feel shame and painfully self-conscious. I remember the feeling of wanting to curl up into a ball and disappear. Then I invite this twelve year old, who is still very much a part of me today, to dance and remember the feelings of lightness and joy.

I imagine myself, as my adult self, joining in the dance with the two young ones. I feel the wonderful, joyful, childlike qualities. As I dance, I feel myself releasing the weight of all that criticism and responsibility. I see the child, growing into a woman, and deserving the chance to blossom and dance to her own rhythm and to discover her own beliefs. My journey continues in this new Dance.

— Jane

Because I have assaulted my mid-life crisis with such an armory, I'm not sure which of the weapons is affecting which change. But I believe that the single hour of creative dancing (sessions) on Monday nights these past months has released something that was bound up in my spirit. Just to dance, to give myself permission to move in any way I feel with minimal attention to others and their opinions, reactions, etc. There was nowhere in my life I did this. This class gave me permission, no, instructed me to dance more in my life. That's why this class is said to be about the inner child. My inner child is dancing more in her life.

I noticed myself dancing in places I didn't before. The night of my very first class I danced in my dream — that wonderful, weightless, leaping, joyful dancing. It was a delicious feeling. I notice myself now just walking down the street and it occurs to me to move in a way that makes it fun or playful — so I let my arms and legs dangle or bounce in a musical rhythm and I dance down the sidewalk or across the parking lot. And several incredibly creative and adventurous ideas have just "come to me" in the last months. I feel the spirit of dance I've let in has made me receptive. I can't wait to see what will happen next!

— Laurel

I can only describe the process when I started "dancing" as the same as the first time I put on diving goggles and stuck my head in the water in Hannama Bay in Hawaii. I had this overwhelming sense of discovery and disbelief. The colors were incredible and I found a whole parallel world that I didn't know existed. I felt the same way when I came to the Movement for the Mind process.

I realized that my body had been recording my experiences and storing them. As I began to explore my life through The Movement for the Mind sessions, I saw that not only was this information from my past stored, but it was also "coloring my world" and affecting all of my behavior and choices.

The process of picking out an experience and dancing with it making it bigger, smaller, twisting it to the left, making it purple or red..... was very freeing. I learned that I could both change my experiences and perceptions, which then allowed me to create different choices in my life.

The painful memories that I had experienced in my past had caused me to disassociate from myself. Through the sessions I re-explored these pieces. At first the process was painful, but then it became peaceful, and was a way of re-claiming parts of myself that I hadn't been comfortable with previously. Connecting to the cut-off parts of myself gave me back a feeling of being truly alive and present in all ways.

When I first started the movement sessions, I was very numb and cut-off. I approached the world from a place where I only allowed people to see a very controlled part of me. I began doing this from a very early age. I had this very limited "face" that I showed to the outside world, therefore, I didn't really know who I was or what I liked or disliked. I began to question my strengths and my challenges, why I was here, and what and whom I cared about. This process allowed me to find the places that I had cut-off and to re-experience them, thereby taking back a part of myself. And I found out that I didn't cease to exist as a result. I found out I wasn't so bad (I also discovered that I wasn't so perfect.) I discovered that I have opinions, dreams and desires. This movement process gave me life.

The two years that I spent intensely doing Movement for the Mind workshops and private session s allowed me to learn about my inner tapestry and to hold on to it. I don't feel the need to work that intensely anymore. However, I do still use it as a meditative, grounding experience to keep me in touch with my inner experiences and to help me work on the areas where I want

*to grow. I've learned that I first have to create space for things on
the inside before I can ever hope to manifest them on the outside.*

— Michelle

*To dance
is to write poetry
with my body
to sing, to laugh,
to fly free.
To rediscover myself,
To be contained
Yet to soar
Through infinite space
Exploring new dimensions
Translating limitations
Into new adventures and visions.
To love myself
To trust,
To speak from the heart,
From the truth
Of my inner being.
To play
And to celebrate life.
To know that I am
Substance, ability, strength
And so much more.
To dance is to be me.*

*I wrote this poem after the art and dance workshop.
Working and expressing through my body in this way has
impacted my life and healing process in a very deep way.*

— Theressa

About the Author

Françoise E. Netter, M.A., President of Body/Mind Dynamics, Inc is an author, columnist, educator, conference presenter, performer and practitioner certification trainer for yoga and Movement for the Mind® throughout the United States, Mexico, and Europe. Françoise has been a leading innovator in the fields of yoga, stress management, body/ mind fitness, dance and movement therapy for over thirty years.

She has taught at numerous universities including Stanford University, Santa Clara University, JFK University, Antioch College, University of Phoenix, University of Colorado and Naropa University. Françoise has trained teachers, therapists, and medical professionals. She currently conducts workshops and graduate credit courses for educators and administrators through Adams State College, Brandman University and California State University, San Bernardino. Her passion is to motivate others and use education as a resource for creativity, inspiration and transformation.

Françoise has been featured on television, radio, several CDs and in magazines and newspapers including *The New York Times, San Francisco Chronicle, San Jose Mercury News* and Health Club Management Magazine. She has a regular column in Circles of Seven Magazine on "Actualizing Your Yoga."

This book offers individuals in all walks of life an opportunity to integrate their creativity—physically, mentally and spiritually— and apply it practically both professionally and personally.

To learn more about Françoise and Body/Mind Dynamics, Inc, or to schedule a workshop, session or practitioner certification training in your area, visit www.bodyminddynamics.org or email fenetter@yahoo.com.

Made in the USA
Middletown, DE
13 November 2022

14665411R00116